LIFE WORLD LIBRARY

THE BALKANS

TIME
LIFE
BOOKS
®

LIFE WORLD LIBRARY

THE BALKANS

by Edmund Stillman

and The Editors of LIFE

TIME INCORPORATED   NEW YORK

COVER: Near the famous bridge of Stari
Most, built by the Turks in Mostar,
Yugoslavia, in the 16th Century,
swimmers sample the cool waters of the
Neretva River. Beyond rise the bleak
limestone mountains of the Dinaric range.

ABOUT THE WRITER

Edmund Stillman, author of the interpretive text for this volume in the
LIFE World Library, is an American writer of widely varied accomplishments. A lawyer with a deep interest in the arts and archeology, he joined
the United States Foreign Service in 1947 and served in Bulgaria and
Yugoslavia. After leaving the Foreign Service in 1951, he became a co-
founder of Walker and Co., a New York publishing house, and a con-
tributor of articles on foreign affairs to a number of U.S. publications. He
is the editor of a collection of essays, poems and stories from the Communist world entitled *Bitter Harvest: The Intellectual Revolt behind the Iron
Curtain,* and co-author, with William Pfaff, of two widely praised studies
of world affairs: *The New Politics* and *The Politics of Hysteria.* Over the
past few years he has made several return visits to Balkan countries.

The Balkans © 1964 Time Inc. All rights reserved. Published simultaneously in Canada.
Revised 1967.
Library of Congress catalogue card number 64-21307.
School and library distribution by Silver Burdett Company.

Contents

TIME-LIFE BOOKS

EDITOR
Maitland A. Edey

TEXT DIRECTOR   ART DIRECTOR
Jerry Korn   Sheldon Cotler

CHIEF OF RESEARCH
Beatrice T. Dobie
Assistant Text Directors:
Harold C. Field, Ogden Tanner
Assistant Art Director: Arnold C. Holeywell
Assistant Chief of Research: Martha Turner

•

PUBLISHER
Rhett Austell
General Manager: Joseph C. Hazen Jr.
Circulation Director: Joan D. Manley
Marketing Director: Carter Smith
Business Manager: John D. McSweeney
Publishing Board: Nicholas Benton, Louis Bronzo,
James Wendell Forbes

LIFE MAGAZINE

EDITOR: Edward K. Thompson
MANAGING EDITOR: George P. Hunt
PUBLISHER: Jerome S. Hardy

LIFE WORLD LIBRARY

SERIES EDITOR: Oliver E. Allen
Editorial Staff for *The Balkans:*
Assistant Editor: Jay Brennan
Designer: Ben Schultz
Writers: Edmund V. White, Peter Wood
Chief Researcher: Grace Brynolson
Researchers: Irene Ertugrul, Evelyn Hauptman, Madeleine Richards,
Ruth Silva, Helen R. Turvey, Rebecca Chaitin, Edward Brash,
Ava Weekes, Paula von Haimberger Arno

EDITORIAL PRODUCTION
Color Director: Robert L. Young
Copy Staff: Marian Gordon Goldman, Helen Isaacs,
Dolores A. Littles
Picture Bureau: Margaret K. Goldsmith, Joan T. Lynch
Art Assistants: James D. Smith, John M. Woods

The text for this book was written by Edmund Stillman, the picture essays by Edmund V. White. Many of the photographs were taken by LIFE staff photographer Carl Mydans. Valuable help was provided by the following individuals and departments of Time Inc.: LIFE staff photographers Alfred Eisenstaedt and Paul Schutzer; LIFE film editor Margaret Sargent; Chief of the LIFE Picture Library Doris O'Neil; Chief of the TIME-LIFE News Service Richard M. Clurman; and Chief of the Bureau of Editorial Reference Peter Draz.

Introduction

The four countries treated in this LIFE World Library volume—Yugoslavia, Albania, Romania and Bulgaria—embrace a region important by any standard. Together, they have a population equal to that of the Middle Atlantic states and New England, with nearly half again the area. Their aggregate human and natural resources are of a high order.

The name Balkan, a Turkish word for mountain, is heard less often than formerly, as the countries more and more are thought of individually. This is good. Traditionally, the Balkan mountains were supposed to separate the maritime civilization to the south from the "barbarians" farther north. This concept derives from a defective knowledge of geography. No less unfortunately, the term Balkan has perpetuated a picture of savage mountains infested with brigands and guerrillas, not to mention vampires. In actual fact, the great rivers and the fertile plains and valleys, where most of the population has always lived, have been —and will remain—far more important.

Unhappily, the Balkan countries lack a tradition of good government. A Serbian proverb says, "At the grave of an official, only donkeys weep." Representative government, introduced after the breakup of the Ottoman Empire, was rarely successful. It was accompanied by revolts and frequently punctuated by dictatorships.

Today the four Balkan countries are under Communist rule. Their regimes differ in detail, but in various essentials all continue to follow the Soviet pattern. Organized opposition, even on the smallest scale, is not tolerated. Police supervision is ubiquitous, although more efficient methods have made it much less evident.

A peasant may be allowed to own a few acres, an artisan may have a tiny shop and a professional man may own his own home. But experience has shown that control is actually more important than ownership. Prices, rentals, credit, property transfers and taxes are subject to rigid control by officials who are hostile to private enterprise of any kind, and against whose rulings there usually is no recourse. In brief, private property and private enterprise, together with the individual liberty stemming from them, have all but disappeared.

There remain, however, considerable accomplishments in industrial development. Much of this development has been achieved at the expense of general living standards, but the net result is still impressive. Again, experience has taught the overriding importance of control, particularly of competent management. The Communist Party in each country continues to fill key positions in all fields with its trusted members, but now requires real ability in addition. The Party hack is placed where he can do no harm.

There remain also the great human resources of the Balkans. Besides millions of sturdy peasants, and a rapidly growing class of workers in production and service industries, there is a large and expanding educated class. The great majority of educated people in the Balkans, moreover, are drawn to the West rather than the East, whatever their avowed politics. The regimes are still dominated in large part by old-line Communists, but they will not be around forever. The next echelon is different. Many foresee more rapid changes for the better when the younger, better educated and more Westernized group can exert a decisive influence.

In this complex of geography, races, history, languages, religions, economics and politics, Edmund Stillman has produced an image of the Balkans which seems to me to be both revealing and fair. The American public will understand this region, and its significance, far better after reading his fascinating book.

KARL LOTT RANKIN
former U.S. Ambassador to Yugoslavia

1

Brave Peoples in a Tragic Region

THE Balkans begin in Istria, the peninsula jutting into the Adriatic Sea on the border of Italy. There the northern Italian landscape of cypress trees, pink and tawny stucco farmhouses and green fields passes shockingly into a savage caricature of itself. It becomes a contorted landscape of barren limestone hills and desolate upland pastures under a light so hard and a sky so piercingly blue that in summer the eye is blinded.

All that is easygoing and prettily charming ends in Italy. Although the huddled mountain towns of Istria, with their stone churches and narrow streets, retain a vaguely Italian look,

where the Balkan zone begins we enter a world of the tragic. Here is an area cut off from the West not so much by distance as by time, a place where the miseries and crimes of the past live on and are a palpable burden. In Istria, life can be very hard; and south and east of Istria, in the heartland of the Balkans, it has been catastrophic in our lifetime.

On the Croatian littoral and in Dalmatia, abutting the dazzling blue of the Adriatic where the tourists swarm today, a mere decade or two ago life was a nightmare—a sentence of doom imposed by the brutality of men. A few miles back of the tourist beaches lie the desolate mountain villages—burned by the armies, Nazi and Communist, native and foreign, that passed this way. Here whole villages were wiped out in an afternoon; the remaining ruins, seemingly old but in reality very new, testify to the chronic afflictions that history has visited on the four Balkan lands—Albania, Yugoslavia, Romania and Bulgaria—that are the subject of this book.

EVEN the natural landscape has the aspect of a lunar hell: great white, lonely peaks, barren of soil or any green, slag and boulders strewn about like the bones of monumental antediluvian beasts. Here for centuries in the pock-marked stone valleys the peasants have grubbed for a bitter livelihood, scooping the life-giving soil from narrow fissures in the rock, carrying it by the basketload to their little walled fields, measuring out their existence in the tiny farms they have cleared in the wastes and tending the gnarled olive trees whose fruit is their only luxury. From these shores generations of Adriatic fishermen have put to sea in the midst of storms—the savage bora blows in late autumn and winter for weeks on end. And still farther southward, in the arid mountains and malarial coastal plains of Albania, life is harsher still, a numbing round of labor amid great deprivation—a harsh material existence overlaid by the political terror imposed by what may well be the most austere brand of Communism in the world today.

Inland of these hostile regions, rural life is only a little better, and it improves only slowly. In the cities—in the old Balkan capitals of Tirana, Albania; Sofia, Bulgaria; Bucharest, Romania; and Belgrade, Yugoslavia—the material improvements brought in this century by the spread of Western technology and learning do not go so deep as to eradicate a kind of ancestral cynicism and doubt which the myriad peoples of the Balkans instinctively feel. There are few Balkan people who cannot be gay at festivals; but there is hardly a Balkan individual who is not at bottom a brooding skeptic. This is the mark of the past. "Balkan" in Turkish means mountain, and the Balkans are the ultimate mountain world—dark, passionate, replete with violence. Much of the Balkans is barren; there are fertile valleys and plains to be sure—but these have been fought over bitterly and have been well watered with blood.

In this southeastern corner of Europe, men and nature have conspired for centuries to make of life a hell. Romans, Goths, Huns, Avars, Slavs, Magyars, Byzantines, Tatars, Turks, Venetians, Austrians, Russians and Germans have all campaigned in these hills—burning and killing. In the Balkans, history is a chronicle of atrocity inflicted by the enemy and atrocity endured by friends. The Balkans are a part of Europe but they are another Europe, disordered, far from prosperous, irrational in their violence. These hills and valleys are Europe's dark and bloody ground. But for the men of the Balkans, the dark and bloody hills and valleys are *their* earth, *their* past, *their* blood, *their* crime, *their* affliction—a sanctified land that is their own.

Other lands are richer and more populous; others have been luckier. In other lands men have tamed life and tried to make it a thing of easy calculation. Not so in the Balkans; there, a few lucky periods aside, men have not prospered for two thousand years and more. There men have been uncommonly brave and strong, and still have been beaten. There men have been industrious and wise—and still have been broken by the terrible reverses of human affairs.

SEEN from a low-orbiting satellite, the Balkan peninsula would appear a tangled network of mountain ranges and valleys; only in the east does the landscape soften in part to a region of flat steppes, which have been disastrously open to invasion and conquest from the east. But geographic descriptions aside, the essential character of the region is difficult to define. The common feature is not linguistic: There are literally dozens of languages and dialects spoken on the peninsula, many of them totally unrelated and incomprehensible a few miles away. The unity is not political surely;

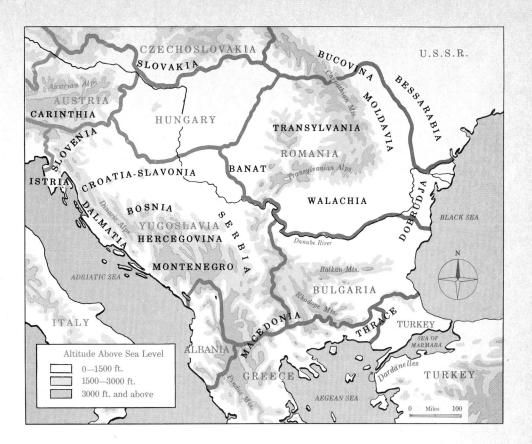

PRINCIPAL REGIONS in the Balkans are indicated in black at right. Holdovers from a time when today's nations did not exist, the regions continue to play a role in Balkan politics and daily life. A man will think of himself primarily as a Serb or a Montenegrin, for example, rather than as a Yugoslav. To some extent, the regions are delimited by mountains and rivers, as in Romania, where Walachia is separated from Transylvania by the Transylvanian Alps and from Dobrudja by the Danube River.

the region today is divided among four hostile and incompatible states.

The region is a kind of minuscule universe. The four modern states stand on the ruins of ancient and medieval empires; they hold within their grasp numbers of diverse and variegated cults and ethnic minorities. In the past, each village or clan has had its art, its dances, its songs, its saints and its passionately proclaimed uniqueness. Only in the last century has the vision of larger national loyalties begun to make headway among the Balkan peoples; even today, attachments to larger units beyond the near horizon can be pitifully weak.

The common features lie elsewhere. They derive perhaps from a common historic experience—the mutual ordeal of the overlordship of foreign powers, the peculiar tensions of a civilization which remains a borderland between Europe and the East. Yet there is, for the outsider, no more striking feature of the life of the Balkans than the commonly shared characteristics of the Balkan peoples—passionately denied by themselves and so frequently negated in history by petty divisions which, in the Balkan lands, have loomed immoderately and

passionately large. Bulgarians, Macedonians, Montenegrins, Romanians—each of these peoples has a dignity, a pride, a passion and a generosity which is touching in the extreme.

Balanced off against the chronic suspicion and expectation of misery is something else: if among these people there is much hate, there is also much love. The British author Rebecca West put it truly when she wrote of the old Balkans that "the mode of life was so honest that it put an end to perplexity. . . . There [was] everything there. Except what we have. But that seems very little."

Yet the reality of the Balkans is the reverse of sentimental. Each of these nationalities would kill any one of the others—and in recent history, each of them has done so with a fierce dedication. Often the social values of these people, the legends they tell, the gods they pray to are the same; but the passionate *difference,* so often barely detectable to the foreign eye, is for these nations the true reality.

This self-conscious diversity within fundamental unity is a major theme of Balkan history. Each of the four nations which make up the modern Balkans knew the centuries-long ordeal of the Turk. Each is an uneasy political entity. Each proclaims a grandiose and messianic destiny and, in one degree or another, continues archaic national policies down to the present day. These similarities are legacies of the still-living past. But the similarities do not end there; more modern ones exist as well. Each of the four remains a predominantly agricultural society; only recently have the nations of the Balkans begun to emerge into 20th Century industrialism.

Each of them, finally, is a Communist state—but each of them is Communist with an intensely felt difference, and there is not one of them that is wholly at ease with the others. Instead, as so often in the troubled past, the four nations (and the component peoples they represent) assert the distinctions. Within the Communist world Albania is an insolent schismatic which has become an enemy of Moscow—and an improbable ally of Red China. Neighboring Yugoslavia is, in Communist parlance, a Right-Wing deviationist—according to Albanian accusers a "capitulationist," "crypto-capitalist" heretic, fast succumbing to the mortal sin of "privatism." Bulgaria, although increasingly restless, remains an appendage of the Soviets—as for years Bulgaria was a satellite of czarist Russia and a tool of its ambitions in the Balkans. Finally, Romania—for so many years that passionately proclaimed "Latin island in a Slavic sea"—now seeks to re-establish ties with Western Europe while cannily asserting neutrality in the bitter Sino-Soviet conflict.

The underlying unities of the region are indisputably real; the divisions exist solely in the

---

A GUIDE TO PRONUNCIATION

There are six major languages in the Balkans: Bulgarian, Serbo-Croatian, Macedonian, Slovenian, Albanian and Romanian. Two of these, Bulgarian and Macedonian, exclusively employ the Cyrillic alphabet, which is also used by Russian. For these two, this volume follows standard practices for transliterating Cyrillic characters into their equivalents in the Latin alphabet used by English. One language—Serbo-Croatian—can be written with either the Cyrillic alphabet or the Latin alphabet (Serbs use the Cyrillic alphabet and Croats employ the Latin). For Serbo-Croatian, and the remaining languages, which use only the Latin alphabet, the editors generally have followed native spellings and retained each language's diacritical marks. In Serbo-Croatian, "š" is pronounced "sh," and "č" is pronounced "ch." "Ć" is also pronounced "ch"; "c" alone is "ts." In Albanian the mark (¨) over an "e" indicates that it should be pronounced like the "a" in "sofa." The letters "xh" are sounded like the "j" in "job." "X" is like the "dz" in "adz." In the Romanian language, "ş" is pronounced "sh" and "ţ" like "ts" in "hats."

---

emotional charge put upon them. But to state the proposition this way is to distort the truth: the divisions are very real because the nations of the Balkans believe them to be so. There are other divisions, to be sure—less illusory ones. The differences in character appear in bold relief after longer acquaintance. The Bulgarians tend to be a kindly, sober, simple, unassuming folk—except when they are roused to inexplicable savagery by nationalist fantasies. "A Bulgarian will hunt a hare in an oxcart—and catch him," runs a Balkan proverb, and, more than most aphorisms, it reflects truth. Yugoslavia's Slovenes, by contrast, are sophisticated, prudent, industrious and technologically advanced. They are little given to romance.

Albanians, like Sicilians, practice the law of vendetta—and the law of blood brotherhood—to the end. Romanians, on the other hand, are a relatively peaceful people, more given to artistic pleasures than to violence. Serbians and their near-relatives, the Montenegrins, are inclined to the quixotic: the romantic, self-destructive gesture is their self-assigned life style.

But generalizations about the Balkans are more than usually dangerous. The Albanians are not one people but two—the northern Ghegs, wild shepherds and mountaineers, and the more placid and reasonable Tosks of the south. The Bosnian Moslem who mourns the decay of Islam, which was brought to the Balkans by the Turkish conquerors, is no Turk: he is descended from the same peoples that his Christian neighbor is. He speaks Serbo-Croatian, not Turkish. Even an essentially homogeneous people like the Bulgarians are riven internally by distinctions of dialect and religion, so that the Orthodox *Shopi*, peasants dwelling in the hills surrounding Bulgaria's capital of Sofia, are alleged to be descendants of the Pecheneg Turks who invaded the Balkans in the 10th Century, and the *Pomaks* are Bulgars who were converted to Islam during the Turkish occupation.

Between the Serbians and the Bulgarians dwell the Macedonian Slavs—an unlucky group of people. They have been called—and forced to be—Bulgarians by Bulgarian military occupiers; they have been called—and forced to be—"South Serbs" by Serbian military occupiers. (The Greeks, not to be outdone, have sought to transform them into Greeks.) The uniform result of all such painful confusions has been blood.

HISTORY has not been kind to the Balkans. The Balkans exist as a permanent rebuke to notions of mechanical betterment. In a sense, they are an antidote to vulgar optimism. They demonstrate all too convincingly that success leads not always to further success but sometimes to disaster. There have been successes in the Balkan past, great empires and great eras of culture, refinement and learning, but they have all been broken by history. All the empires have gone down to defeat; all the lucky seasons have faded.

The Balkan nations know the lesson of their past all too well: transience and failure are great themes in Balkan literature and art. Failure is the theme of the greatest of the medieval epics of the Balkan peoples, *Ballad of Kosovo*, which celebrates not victory but defeat by the Turk—their choosing, so they say, of a spiritual rather than a worldly kingdom. The rejection of the material world is also the essential theme of the Manichaean heretics, the Bogomils, who held part of these lands so long in defiance of the Eastern and Western churches, denying the holiness of creation and asserting that the earth is the botched work of the devil. Mutability of fortune is an essential theme of that earlier Balkan people, the ancient Greeks, who, as the historian Arnold Toynbee has

written, were "haunted . . . by the possibilities of disaster inherent in success of every kind, in personal prosperity, in military victory, in the social triumph of civilization [itself]."

This has been their lesson, but it is a lesson which, curiously, the surrounding world has blindly ignored. There is no more inexplicable feature of the Balkan past than the readiness of the Balkans' larger, more populous and happier neighbors to plunge into the Balkan maelstrom—and by so doing bring about their own destruction. The miseries of Balkan history might have remained for the most part parochial catastrophes—a human tragedy but not a world-wide affliction—had the great states of Europe left the region to itself.

They could not do so: the Balkan political turmoils exerted a deadly fascination. For the great powers, these chronic disturbances and conflicts held out for each a fancied opportunity for empire. Yet there is not a great power which has intervened in the Balkans and been the better for it: witness the tragic lesson of the First and Second World Wars. This is the lesson given us by the rebuke administered to Soviet imperialism in the Balkans today: all the vast military and economic power of the Soviet Union, all its menace and bluster, have not been sufficient to control the passions and discords endemic to this tiny corner of Europe. Here, Soviet claims to preside over a universal empire have been challenged and compromised —by states only the merest fraction of the Soviet Union in size—and the Soviets have been forced to endure the rebuke.

THUS the themes of Balkan history repeat and repeat seemingly endlessly. The Balkans are a warning. And for those who believe that 10 years in the life of a nation constitute an eon, who believe that national prestige, power and prosperity endure in the unalterable scheme of things, they are a deadly warning. The Balkans are the reverse of facile American optimism. They teach us that everything passes, everything breaks, everything fades.

In Bucharest, the capital of Romania, a soldier and a peasant woman make up part of the crowd. Once compared to Paris, Bucharest

Actors Who Yearn
to Seize the Stage

The Balkan countries have provided a setting for countless conflicts throughout history, but have seldom been able to assume a leading role. Situated at a political and geographic crossroads, the small nations have played critical

today is a changing city, but with few cars on its broad avenues.

COMMUTING LABORERS, who reside in the surrounding countryside because of an urban housing shortage, flood the Bucharest railroad station as they come to work in the morning.

SHADED PARK, one of many for which Sofia, Bulgaria, is noted *(below)*, provides a pleasant locale for urbanites to engage in the Southern European custom of sitting and gossiping.

roles in the fierce dramas of two continents and have often been crushed in the fray. Despite these defeats, each country yearns for the limelight. Restless, passionate and proud, the Balkan peoples long to determine their own fate.

A POTENTIAL BUYER looks over some ducks in the marketplace at Pleven, a northern Bulgarian city. Bicycles and motorbikes like those in the background are the usual transportation in both Bulgaria and Romania.

A WARM EMBRACE between a mother and daughter in a Sofia slum typifies close family feeling in Bulgaria. These slums are particularly run-down, lacking all conveniences such as indoor toilets and running water.

A QUIET STREET leading through the village of Pitau in Romania is disturbed only by the noise of a farmer's cart and horse. The church in the background is identifiable as Orthodox by the shape of the dome and cross.

STILL WATERS of Lake Scutari, the largest lake on the Balkan peninsula, lie between Yugoslavia and Albania. Rough, jagged mountains like these run parallel to Yugoslavia's entire coast.

PLUNGING WATERFALLS roar *(left)* below a ruined hilltop fortress *(background)* at Jajce in Bosnia, Yugoslavia. Jajce was the seat of the Bosnian kings in the 14th and 15th Centuries.

REMOTE TOWN, Kotor clings to the steep side of Mount Lovćen on the Montenegrin coast of Yugoslavia. Surrounded by water and cliffs, Kotor never fell to raiding Ottoman Turks.

WADING GEESE track in the mud near the fishing boats of the small Romanian village of Sfîntu Gheorghe in the delta land, a vast region formed by the three arms of the Danube.

SUN-BROWNED BOYS head for the Neretva River *(below)* in Mostar, Yugoslavia. The Turks, who once ruled all of Herce-govina from Mostar, filled the city with handsome buildings.

FRUGAL HOUSEWIFE puts the wash out to dry on the grass in her backyard in Moldavia. Peasants generally consider a clothesline an unnecessary luxury. Moldavia, one of the two original principalities that formed the Old Kingdom of Romania a hundred years ago, is a region which is rich in corn and wheatlands bordering on Bessarabia in the Soviet Union.

2

Vanished Splendors

I AM safely arrived at the end of my very long journey," wrote Lady Mary Wortley Montagu, wife of the ambassador of His Majesty George I to the court of the Grand Turk. She wrote her dear friend and confidante, Mrs. Thistlethwayte, in the spring of 1717 from Adrianople, where the Turkish sultan was then holding court. Exhausted by an arduous journey southeastward from civilized Vienna, then the glittering capital of the Habsburgs, she could hardly bear to recall the details of her ordeal, although she was normally an irrepressible spirit and a person of lively and enquiring mind. "I will not tire you with the account of

the many fatigues I have suffered," she concluded, turning instead to more amusing topics —the camels (". . . . 'Tis a particular art to load them, because of the bunch on their backs. They seem to me very ugly . . .") and the interior furnishings of a Turkish harem.

Lady Mary's tedious route had crossed the desolate and war-devastated plain between the Austrian capital and Belgrade, then only a small city which commanded the confluence of the Danube and Sava Rivers and which the Turkish military governor used for his court. From Belgrade her route led to the southeast again, through the brigand-infested forests and hill country of Serbia to the town of Niš, through the valley of the Nišava to Sofia, and finally from Philippopolis on the southern Balkan plain to Adrianople.

The Grand Turk kept a great estate in Adrianople, but Lady Mary reported the Balkan lands to the north were barren and poor. The villagers all seemed rogues: dirty, lazy, thieving ruffians. The ubiquitous pigs ran wild—pork was one meat the avaricious Turks would not seize from the despised rayah, or non-Moslem subjects—and they rooted in the sewage and village mud. Along the road one met herds of shambling water buffalo—black, evil-smelling beasts with wicked white eyes—and troops of Turkish *spahis,* or cavalrymen, on patrol. At the crossroads there might be built a gibbet. There the corpses of haiduks—the ever-present highwaymen of the 18th Century Balkans— were exposed in futile warning to their comrades. It was a desolate land given over, it seemed, to impenetrable ignorance and decay.

Yet it had not always been so. The Adrianople from which Lady Mary wrote her friends had been, she knew, in Roman days a strategically important city, founded with expectations of grandeur by the Emperor Hadrian. Sofia, a small town which she found "beautiful," had, as Sardica, vied once with Byzantium for the honor of becoming the Empire's second Rome. Near Niš, the Emperor Constantine the Great had been born. The outlandish Philippopolis had been the city of the redoubtable King Philip II of Macedon, father of Alexander the Great.

IN the dusty fields near Adrianople, the Roman Empire had gone down to defeat before the Goths, and again, some eight centuries later, shortly after the Fourth Crusade, the flower of European chivalry had been humbled by the mailed horsemen of Kaloyan, self-styled emperor of an until-then-unknown Empire of the Bulgars and Vlachs. There had been other empires in these obscure regions: those, for example, of the Serbian autocrats Milutin and Stefan Dušan, who had constructed great churches and given humane laws; of the great Bulgarian czars Simeon and Samuel, who had threatened Constantinople itself; of the Romanian Prince Michael the Brave, who had briefly united Moldavia, Walachia and Transylvania against both Habsburgs and Turks.

YET, by Lady Mary Wortley Montagu's day —only a century after Michael the Brave's death—the very memory of these great deeds and empires had all but passed away. The memory remained only in the distorted folk legends of the downtrodden peasantry or in the smoke-blackened and ill-understood frescoes that illuminated the interiors of crumbling churches and monasteries. It was only in the 19th Century, under the impact of new ideas slowly penetrating from the West, that the true memory was revived. The splendors of ancient and medieval times were rediscovered by Serbian, Croatian, Slovene, Bulgarian, Romanian and Greek folklorists, archeologists and historians —and, regrettably, by Balkan politicians and propagandists.

For nations like the Balkan states, hemmed in by powerful and rapacious enemies, a sense of national identity is an absolute condition of survival; but the old Balkan stories in the second half of the 19th Century and the first half of the 20th bequeathed more than a salutary national pride in a long-forgotten tradition. In the heated crucible of Balkan politics and great power rivalries, these traditions of empire and glory became too often mere rationalizations for bloody national combats, for grandiose claims and counterclaims to one or another disputed province or city. Ambitious politicians stirred up national fanaticism. Peoples who had experienced the common ordeal of Turkish oppression and who—like Serbs and Bulgarians— shared a common culture were set against each other. The old battles were refought, and the blood spilled centuries before was spilled again.

The origins of the turbulent Balkan peoples are lost in the mists of time. To this strategically located region, early man penetrated out of Asia, establishing farming and herding communities. Almost from the beginning the area was a racial potpourri. The Danubian plain —in which lie most of present-day Romania, northern Bulgaria, northeast Yugoslavia and most of Hungary as well—is the westernmost bay of the great Asiatic steppe; where mountains like the Balkans, the Dinaric Alps, or the Carpathians block the plain, rivers breach the geographical barrier. The Danube especially has funneled wandering tribesmen and itinerant traders along what has been throughout history a great highway of races.

TO the early Greeks, who preferred the sea and only with great reluctance penetrated inland, the Balkan hinterlands were largely unknown. In succeeding centuries, the Greeks established small trading cities along the Adriatic and Black Sea coasts.

By Greece's Golden Age—the Fifth Century B.C.—parts of the area were well enough known to dispel the darkest legends. The region at that time was well forested and fruitful. Greek ways of thought and life slowly penetrated; by the day of Philip of Macedon, when Greece had already entered on its age of decline, it was the hill kings of Macedonia who fell heir to the military and cultural legacy that was rightfully Greece's own. Aristotle went north to tutor Philip's precocious son Alexander, and Philip himself, contemptuously overriding the divided opposition that Demosthenes could muster among the demoralized Greek states, conquered the Greek peninsula in 338 B.C.

Under Alexander's inspired leadership, Macedonia achieved its own golden age. Pausing only to consolidate the royal succession and to subdue the wild and formidable Thracian and Illyrian tribes who dwelt to his north, Alexander rallied his armies of Macedonian pikemen. (The Macedonian *sarissa* was an impressive weapon, 14 to 21 feet long, so that the phalanx in motion looked like a monster hedgehog.) With his Greek allies, he plunged across the Hellespont, the frontier between Europe and Asia, to take the ancient, luxurious and by now degenerate empire of the Persians by storm.

Between the years 334 and 323 B.C., Alexander marched through the Levant, Egypt and Central Asia, breached the barrier of the Hindu Kush and stared down on the plains of India. An alliance with the Indian prince Porus hardly survived his death, and the Macedonian garrisons were expelled. Throughout southwestern Asia the legend survives to this day of "Iskander," a distant folk memory of the ambitious Balkan prince who convulsed the whole ancient world, wanted to become a god, and died at the age of 33. Alexander left a son; but he left ambitious captains as well. They fell to quarreling over his inheritance, and the empire Alexander had built was carved up among them and their successors.

A century and a half after Alexander's death another power took the offensive in the Balkans. In 168 B.C. Rome conquered and annexed the Adriatic kingdom of Illyria; by 9 A.D. the Empire had extended its control to the Danube. As Rome advanced into the imperial age, an unprecedented era of civilization and security began for the Balkans. Great cities were built and great roads were constructed, like the Via Egnatia, that ran from what is today Durrës in Albania and across the Albanian Alps to Salonika and Constantinople. Trade flourished, although in Apuleius' charming Roman novel, *The Golden Ass,* the Balkans were still the haunt of brigands and witches. But civilization advanced—and with it the slave system and the cruelty that marred the Roman social landscape.

THE proud Balkan peoples refused to submit tamely. When the wild Dacians, under their great leader Decebalus, menaced Rome's Danubian provinces, Rome launched a fierce counteroffensive. Between 101 and 107 A.D., they conquered the northern bank of the Danube, bringing the whole area into the orbit of Roman politics and culture.

There are ample archeological remains to attest the level of Roman culture in the region in those centuries. While for us, the Roman imprint on the West looms largest, it may be that

25

in the early centuries of our era the center of Roman imperial life lay in these Eastern regions. Certainly as the centuries of Roman rule wore on, the military center of gravity shifted more and more to the East—not only because the barbarian tribes who menaced the Empire came from the East, but because the Balkan provinces of the Empire supplied the troop levies to keep these invaders at bay.

In an age of declining order and the supremacy of ambitious military politicians—politicians made and unmade by the increasingly undisciplined legions—the Balkan provinces came to supply emperors as well. Some of these played minor roles. Others, like Diocletian, who was born on the Adriatic coast near what is today the Yugoslav seaport of Split, restored the cohesion and stability of the Empire. Perhaps the most influential of all was Constantine the Great, the emperor who made Christianity his own faith and gave it the active support of the Empire.

It may be, as the historian Edward Gibbon would have it, that these years of the high noon of the Roman Empire were the happiest of mankind's history. Certainly for the Balkans, despite the social blight of slavery and the weight of Roman taxation, they were an unwonted period of prosperity and peaceful advance in the arts of living. But the idyl was soon to end; for all the heroic efforts of the Eastern emperors, the Roman sun was about to set.

THE barbarian pressures against the Roman frontiers grew year by year. Far to the east, in lands that were only legend to the Roman provincials, the great Chinese empire of the Han administered a crushing defeat to an Asian tribe known as the Hsiung-nu in the First Century A.D. These people were the ancestors of the fierce Asiatic tribes who enter our history 300 years later as the Huns. They and other barbarian peoples—Ostrogoths, Visigoths and Alans—spelled the death of the old classical world. Dacia north of the Danube, the modern Romania, was the province nearest the storm center, and it was the first province of

the Empire to give way before the onslaught.

The Roman legions withdrew from Dacia in 275, evacuating many of the provincials to comparative safety south of the new Danube frontier, but abandoning the rest to their fate. Many died but others took to the hills with their flocks—and their Latin language—to reappear centuries later as ancestors of the modern Romanians. The respite to Rome was short, however. By the Fourth Century the pressure could hardly be contained, and in ensuing centuries the barbarians burst completely through the frontiers. Goths, Huns and Avars overran the Balkan provinces, bringing the laboriously built culture of the region to ruin. These were dark times, and it may be that they were darkest of all in these southeastern provinces of Rome. But from the forgotten tragic years of the Fifth, Sixth, Seventh and Eighth Centuries the ethnic and linguistic map of the modern Balkan states takes its origin.

IN the west of the Balkans, in what had been the Roman province of Illyricum, named for the native Illyrians, the language of the ancient inhabitants had been preserved through the years of Roman domination, although the local speech had been influenced by Latin. In the highlands, what is today Albania, this language was preserved essentially intact. The modern Albanians—*Shqipëri*, or "Sons of the Eagle," they call themselves—are descendants of the tribes who held these wild mountains before recorded history began.

On the frontiers of Albania began the zone of the Slavs. They had originated far to the north and the east, but they had slowly drifted south in the wake of the more terrible Goths, Huns and Avars. The ancestors of the modern Serbs, Croats, Slovenes, Macedonians and Bulgarians, the Slavs thus enter the pages of history quietly. They were a slow, stolid, farming and pastoral people, at first worshiping pagan gods like Perun, the thunder, and wood spirits and mountain *vile*, or nymphs.

East of the Dinaric Alps they took vast areas, although some historians (and in the Balkans,

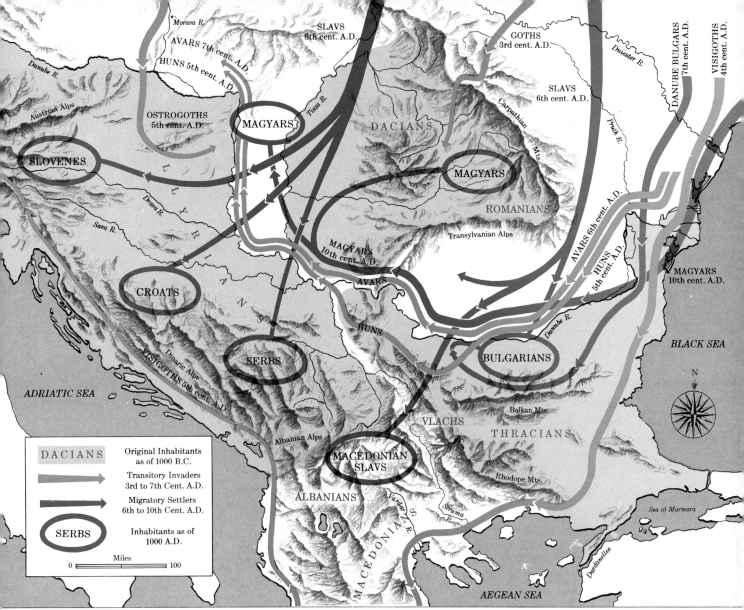

THE MOVEMENTS OF PEOPLES through the Balkans over a 2,000-year period are shown above. Into an area originally inhabited by the Illyrians, Thracians and Dacians *(light-green tone)* came two types of invaders: raiders like the Goths, Huns and Avars *(light-green lines)* who passed through the area and did not stay, and migrants like the Slavs, Magyars and Danube Bulgars *(dark-green lines)* who entered between the Sixth and 10th Centuries A.D. and settled in the areas indicated by circles, becoming known as Croats, Serbs and the like. These incursions displaced the original inhabitants, whose descendants however remain today: the Illyrians can be traced to today's Albanians, the Thracians to the Vlachs, the Dacians to the Romanians.

where history can be a convenient rationale for political atrocity or racial murder, history is not an objective calling) more contemptuously have likened their descent into the region to the seeping of water through earth. Be that as it may, it is clear that in the early history of Europe the Slavs appear more often as victims of other invaders than as aggressors.

Thrust into this zone of Slavic dominance was the Hungarian kingdom established in the Ninth Century by the Magyars, a wild horse people from the Central Asian steppes. By moving into what is now Hungary, the Magyars separated the southern Slavs from the more numerous Slavs who occupied what is today Poland and Czechoslovakia, on the one hand, and the Ukraine and Russia on the other. Elsewhere—in Macedonia, in northern Greece, in the hills behind the Adriatic coast—were pockets of Vlachs, or Aromani; these were descendants of the Romanized colonials who had taken to the hills to escape the barbarian hordes and

27

had gradually lapsed into barbarism themselves.

Farthest east of the major peoples to be drawn into this Balkan maelstrom were the Bulgars, a people related to the earlier Hun invaders of the region. In the Seventh and Eighth Centuries they had ridden out of the eastern steppes, occupying northern territories of the Byzantine Empire, as the Greek-speaking successor to the Roman Empire was known.

The Bulgars were horse-archers on the classic Central Asian model. Under their great Khan Asperukh, these warrior nomads established an ascendancy over the Slavic tribesmen who dwelt in the east Balkan lands between the Danube and the Balkan mountain range. By the opening years of the Ninth Century, they were powerful enough to challenge the Byzantine Empire itself: in 811 A.D. they shattered a Byzantine army sent against them, slaying the Emperor Nicephorus I in battle and (a Balkan touch) making a wassail cup of his skull. But for all their wild ways, the Bulgars soon interbred with their more numerous Slav subjects and adopted Slavic language and customs. The result was a mixed race speaking a language almost wholly Slavic in its structure and vocabulary.

For a few centuries the Roman Empire, in the new guise of the Greek-speaking Byzantines, had been able to restore imperial authority in the peninsula as the worst furies of the barbarian invasions passed. To this day the Balkan nations refer to Constantinople (now Istanbul) as Tsarigrad, "the Emperor's City." Mindful of the rapacity and envy of its manifold enemies, Constantinople was then the most cultivated city in the world, together with Moslem Baghdad and Cordova a beacon in the darkness. But the growth of the Bulgarian state

---

THE DISPUTED ORIGIN OF "SLAV"

The origin of the name of the Slavs, the tribal ancestors of so many of the Balkan peoples, and of the Poles and Russians as well, has been considerably disputed. The dispute, moreover, is a partial reflection of the tensions between peoples which have long permeated the area. The Slavs themselves offer a totally legendary explanation, tracing the origin of the name to *slava*, the word for "glory" in the ancient Slavic language. Some philologists connect the word with the medieval Latin word *sclaveni*, from which the English word "slave" is derived. Still another suggestion sometimes offered is that the word derives from a river or swampy area known as "Slava" or "Slova." The Slavic peoples did, in fact, originally come from the marshy regions of the upper Vistula valley area in what is today Poland.

---

in the Ninth Century threatened to upset this restored Roman-Byzantine glory.

The situation was worsened, not helped, by the conversion of the pagan Bulgarians to Christianity. In 863 A.D., the Byzantine emperor had sent the two brothers Cyril and Methodius to convert the Slavs of Moravia. They brought great qualities of intelligence and devotion to the task—for one thing devising an alphabet (from which was derived the present alphabet of the Bulgarians, Serbs and Russians, now called the Cyrillic). But central Europe was far distant from Byzantine power. Because of the opposition of the Frankish-German Roman Catholic Church in Moravia, the missionary effort failed. But the disciples of the two "Slavonic Apostles" migrated southward and introduced the Slavic liturgy to the Bulgarians. In 870 the Bulgarian king, Boris, made Orthodox Christianity the state religion. But in the process of conversion to Orthodoxy, there existed a fatal flaw. The Bulgar monarchs might wish to adopt the superior culture—and the faith—of their polished Byzantine neighbors, but they could not wish to submit to the arrogant authority of the emperor in his gilded palace in Constantinople. Yet the Orthodox faith in theory recognized no higher authority than that of the emperor; the patriarch of Constantinople might quarrel with the pope, but the patriarch could not gainsay the authority of the Byzantine emperor. For religion in the Eastern Empire was subordinate to the state, and the Bulgar king, when he accepted the new faith, was in the eyes of the Eastern emperors accepting a vassalage to Byzantium as well.

For a proud Bulgarian monarch like Simeon the Great, a man who at the beginning of the

10th Century ruled a great empire stretching from the Danube delta to the Adriatic, no such vassalage was tolerable. His ambition, on the contrary, was to supplant the emperor himself in Constantinople. Thus began a great, century-long struggle between the Bulgarian state and the glittering Byzantine civilization.

IN this protracted conflict between Byzantium and its most brilliant offspring—for the Bulgarians, in their capital at Preslav and later at Turnovo, had attained a level of culture far exceeding that of the contemporary English, Germans or French—no one could win. While the Bulgarians struggled with the Byzantines, new waves of invaders—Russians and Pechenegs—struck at their rear and overran their lands. The result inevitably was the ruin of Bulgaria's fortunes. In 976, a Bulgarian rebel who styled himself the Great Czar Samuel might rise in revolt and establish an ephemeral Bulgarian empire; but in 1014 a Byzantine army would put his forces to rout. The Byzantines are said to have taken 14,000 prisoners in the field and to have blinded 99 out of every 100 in yet another atrocity. Samuel, the story goes, died of a broken heart when he saw them, and Bulgarian national hopes died with him as well. Four years later, the defeated Bulgarian state was made a Byzantine province. Yet the conflict was in the end to affect Byzantine fortunes as well, since, encouraged by this distraction on Byzantium's western and northern frontiers, the other enemies of the Empire (the Seljuk Turks and the Venetians among them) began to press forward.

While Bulgaria lost in the 11th Century, others seemed to gain. Westernmost in the Balkans lay the cultivated Byzantine-Slav trading cities like Zara (today's Zadar), Traù (Trogir) and Ragusa (Dubrovnik), which carried on a thriving commerce with the Moslem East. Here, a graceful and aristocratic native culture was born, but it was all too short-lived as one by one these lovely cities fell under the power of Venice and a mixed Dalmatian-Venetian culture took its place. Inland, the kingdom of

the Croats fell under the power of the Hungarian state.

Their cousins the Serbs were luckier. A Slavic people, the Serbs had hitherto cut no great figure in the Balkan turmoils, but with the collapse of the Bulgarian kingdom and the weakening of the hegemony of Byzantine emperors, their fortune was to be made. Under the powerful Serbian kingdom for more than two centuries, from the 13th to the 15th, there was in the southern and western Balkans an efflorescence of culture impressive by any standards. The Nemanjić kings (as the ruling house was known) promulgated enduring laws, founded monasteries, encouraged learning and left a glowing legacy (see Chapter 8) in the visual arts which endures to this day.

The greatest of these Serbian kings was Stefan Dušan—one of those glorious figures in history, like Solomon after the more austere David, whose very power, pomp and glory catch the imagination of posterity but who seem to mask the incipient decline of the nations they rule. In 1355, Dušan was contending with the Hungarian king for the hegemony of the Balkans when word reached him of the abdication of the Byzantine emperor. Supplanting the emperor had been, we have seen, the persistent dream of each of the Balkan principalities, and Dušan turned his back on the Balkan adventure close at hand; marching east to do battle before Constantinople. But he died before he could realize his ambition, and with him the Serbian state disappeared. He was succeeded by nonentities, and, as has so often been the case in Balkan history, a great and showy empire collapsed leaving scarcely a trace.

THE Balkans were now the arena of warring princes, each unequal to his inheritance. But even in the great days, it is doubtful that the Balkan kingdoms and empires—with the possible exception of the Byzantine state—had ever been able to exercise more than a restraining authority over the local officials and boyars, the great landowners who owed nominal vassalage to kings and emperors. Where there was gross misgovernment, despair among the people deepened. A striking feature of the Balkan social scene in the three or four hundred years after the conversion of the Slavs was the growth of religious heresies. Chief and most interesting of these was the heretical Christian sect of the Bogomils—the Beloved of God—meek, sober men and women who held that the flesh was corruption and the world itself the creation of Satan.

The Bogomils discouraged marriage, abjured this world and preferred the next. This last wish was one that was fulfilled for them in full measure, as the Eastern and Western churches co-operated for once in stamping out a movement hateful to both. Yet despite savage persecution, the movement continued to gain strength.

By the middle of the 14th Century, the Balkan lands were thus sunk in political decay, religious conflict and social disorder. No region can long endure such schisms, least of all one situated on the high road of history. Eastward of Constantinople lay the Turks.

THE latest of the repeated waves of conquest mounted out of Central Asia, the Turks were perhaps in purely military terms the most efficient. Under a series of brilliant sultans, they had swarmed out of the steppes and made their fortunes by lopping off province after province of the enfeebled Byzantine state. By the middle of the 14th Century, one of their clans, the Ottoman, had grown immensely powerful. The Byzantine rulers, existing only by exercise of a wily but precarious diplomacy, planted the Ottoman Turks on the European shore in 1349 to act as a buffer against Serbian ambitions. But when Stefan Dušan died in 1355, the Turks remained.

The Turks expanded conquest by conquest through the Balkan peninsula. In 1371 they defeated the Serbians on the Maritsa River, and the way to total hegemony in the Balkans seemed open. The great, and final, test of strength between the heirs of the Nemanjić hegemony and the Turks came on the Field of Blackbirds—Kosovo Polje—on June 28, 1389.

The Serbian czar, Lazar, the old legend has it, was visited on the eve of battle by the prophet Elijah, and was offered an earthly kingdom or a heavenly one. The pious Lazar chose salvation, but at the price of condemning his people to a centuries-long agony. The two armies—the Balkan Christian confederation and the Ottoman Turks—met in battle the next morning. The result for the Serbs was final defeat.

THE Turkish sultan, Murat, was murdered, in obscure circumstances, by a Serbian renegade or deserter while he waited for news of the battle in his tent. But if the intention of the assassin was to help the cause of the Christian armies, the result was the reverse. Murat died only to be succeeded by his son Bayezid, surnamed the Thunderbolt. While Bayezid some years later was himself defeated in battle by the Asian war lord Tamerlane the Great, and exhibited by that prince in an iron cage, such was the vigor and recuperative power of the Ottoman state that within a few years the Turks had returned to the offensive. (In 1453 they were to take Constantinople itself.) One by one the now feeble Balkan Christian states fell to the Turks. The Turkish armies forayed across the Danube, threatened the trading cities of the coast and defeated the armies of the Austrian and Hungarian states.

Inland there was silence. The great Balkan culture of the preceding centuries was snuffed out. For the Balkan Christian peoples this was a new experience. Invaders had come before, but each time they had been assimilated and converted. The Turks, however, were armed with the proud faith of Islam. The rayah were everywhere despised, if not always badly treated. Conditions of political order might improve; but now the Balkan peoples were aliens in their own land. This was national degradation, an end to dreams of national glory. For 500 years the Balkan peoples—Bulgarians, Albanians, Greeks, Serbs, Romanians—groaned under this weight of alien rule. *"Pod igoto,"* they called it in their songs and brigands' ballads —"under the yoke."

A brightly kerchiefed peasant woman milks a cow in the desolate Velika Strana Mountains of Montenegro in southern Yugoslavia.

Patterns Surviving despite Endless Exploitation

Dominated by Rome and Byzantium, overwhelmed by the Ottoman Turks or manipulated by Austria, Hungary and Russia, the Balkan peasant has survived to witness each of his foreign masters thwarted. Although history reflects continuing exploitation, one aspect of Balkan life endures through the vagaries of conquest and defeat, poverty and prosperity: the rural existence. The institution which preserved that existence over the centuries was the *zadruga*, a community of farmers closely related and owning property in common. The cooperatives begun in the 1890s and the collective farms of today are partly outgrowths of the *zadruga*. By sharing labor and equipment, Balkan peasants eke out a living amid persisting adversity.

SCYTHING GRASS, three Moslem farmers clear a meadow in Bosnia-Hercegovina, Yugoslavia, where the influence of Turkish rule still prevails, and there are nearly a million Moslems.

THRESHING GRAIN on a Bulgarian cooperative farm, a worker drives his horses over oat stalks. Although they are predominantly Slavic, Bulgarians have traces of Central Asian blood.

HARVESTING WHEAT, a Slovene and his wife gather grain on their own farm. While he uses a special scythe that keeps the stalks from scattering, she bundles the fallen grass into sheaves.

INDEPENDENCE gained from familiar ways is a hallmark of the peasantry

A BIBLICAL FIGURE, a Romanian shepherd boy dressed in the costume of eastern Transylvania guards his flock, in a scene that is reminiscent of ancient days, as his sheep slowly move down from their summer pastures in the mountains. Although collectivization has driven many farmers to the cities, shepherds still hold onto their primitive and virtually autonomous lives.

COOPERATIVE FARMS *yield the corn and wheat which feed the peninsula*

PREPARING FODDER, Romanians rake cornstalks on a collective in the lower Danube valley. The corn is fed into the machine in the background, which grinds it into silage for storing.

PLOWING STUBBLE on the Thracian Plain in southern Bulgaria, adolescent boys drive tractors as part of their training course in modern agricultural methods on a cooperative farm.

IN CLOSE BANDS, farm people work with the same mutual assistance practiced by their ancestors

LUNCH BREAK on a Bulgarian collective *(right)* supplies farmers with an opportunity to repair scythes on spikes driven into the earth. Their lunch consists of cucumbers, turnips and bread.

EXCLUSIVE GROUP manning a threshing machine in Transylvania *(opposite)* are all related. The Transylvanians long fought collectives, and most still prefer working together in family teams.

SEGREGATED CIRCLE of women *(below)* dozes and drinks water from a wicker-covered jar. Although they work with the men in the top picture, the women stay together during rest periods.

*A HOG BREEDER lives comfortably
and earns an independent
income on a Serbian cooperative*

FAMILY PORTRAIT shows Dušan Serdar with his wife, children and mother before the house he built on his farm near Belgrade, Yugoslavia. The farm is part of a *zadruga*, or cooperative.

EVENING MEAL of peppers and goat cheese brings the Serdar family together in their kitchen-living room. Serdar's mother keeps house so that his wife can be free to help on the farm.

PROUD OWNER, Dušan Serdar brings an armload of feed to one of his 40 hogs. Serdar must purchase all his feed from the *zadruga*, but he is free to sell his pork elsewhere if he chooses.

FATTENED SWINE are cared for by Serdar's hired hand. In 1945 the *zadruga* started Serdar and 2,500 other peasants in pig raising by supplying each man with two hogs for breeding.

Wearing the distinctive Moslem headgear, a man of Krujë, an Albanian mountain town, talks with a friend. It was from Krujë that the

national hero, Skanderbeg, fought the Turks in the 15th Century.

3

Conquest, Anarchy and War

IF any single factor made the Balkans what they were in history—and what they still are today—it was the ordeal of the Turk. But just what the 500 years of Turkish occupation meant to the Balkans is no easy matter to define. The image of the Turk has undergone radical transformation three times in modern history. For us in the mid-20th Century, the image of Turkey is that of a staunch ally of the West against the Soviets and of a modern state which is the legacy of Mustafa Kemal, the first and in some degree the most ambitious of the modernizers of the Islamic tradition. But that is an image which dates only from the years after World War I and World War II. For the 18th and 19th Centuries, the image of Turkey was that of a rotting empire, of a corrupt, incompetent and sadistic national elite preying on the subject Balkan peoples—of a cynical government whose very method of rule was atrocity. And for still earlier times the image of the Turk was one of power—stark, inexorable and menacing to Europe. For as Martin Luther said in the 16th Century, "The Turks are the people of the wrath of God."

Each of these images is in some measure true—for its time. What is indisputable is that each of the earlier Turkeys had a perceptibly different impact on the Balkans. The effect on the Balkans of the Turkish occupation in the years of Ottoman power, stability and glory was one thing, but in the long years of decay and humiliation it was quite another. This is the story we must now briefly trace.

BECAUSE both Lazar, the leader of the Balkan confederation, and Murat, the Sultan of the Turks, had died when the Balkan forces were defeated at Kosovo in 1389, there was for some years afterward uncertainty in Europe about the significance of the battle. Church bells, so the story goes, were rung in Paris in rejoicing for the defeat of the "seed of Ismael," as the Turks were known. But the reality was the reverse. The power of the Balkan Christian states declined steadily after 1389; the power of the Turks grew. In 1453 they seized Constantinople from Constantine XI, last of the weakened Byzantine emperors. Soon they were threatening Western Europe as well: In 1480 Turkish troops seized Otranto in southern Italy, and in 1499 patrols raided the outskirts of Venice and Vicenza. In 1526 the Turkish armies destroyed the power of the Hungarian state, occupying all but the westernmost strip of the country, which sought the protection of Austria, and three years later they besieged the great city of Vienna itself.

The Turkish achievement in those years was not merely a military one. Whatever the glory of the medieval Balkan principalities may have been before the tragedy of Kosovo, conditions of order had already begun to break down in the Balkans before the Turks ever came. On an economic and social level, the decline of central authority in these medieval states had led to the growth of the power of feudal barons and the consequent degradation and impoverishment of the peasantry. But there

had been more than an economic and social oppression by the secular power. There was a parallel religious intolerance and oppression of schismatics like the Bogomils.

Thus, for the peasants and the schismatics, the coming of the Turk, for all the savagery of the onslaught, was not an unmitigated tragedy. In the first centuries of Turkish rule, conditions of public order markedly improved; the Turks, contrary to the commonly held myth of the fanatical warriors of Islam, practiced a religious toleration remarkable for that or any age. Christians and Jews, in the eyes of the followers of the Koran, were like themselves "people of the book"; their option was to convert to Islam or not as they chose, as long as they paid a head tax incumbent on all nonbelievers.

As for the persecuted Bogomils, many of them found in the austere religion of the Koran striking parallels to their own creed. Conversion for them was no terrible matter. Persecuted by Orthodox and Catholics alike, they swung their allegiance to the Turks in 1463 and opened the gates of Bosnia. (It is from this act of apostasy that the vast majority of Moslems in the western Balkans derive. They are linguistically and racially akin to their Christian neighbors, rather than to the Turks.)

The truth is that the Turks were largely indifferent in matters of religion, although, fearing that the religions of their subjects might serve as focal points of resistance, they forbade the building of all but the meanest churches, and likewise outlawed the ringing of church bells.

WHAT was damaging to the Balkan peoples was something else: They had been stripped of pride and freedom. As Christians, they were now despised. While any subject boy might aspire to the highest rank in the Turkish Empire, he had to convert to Islam to do so; when the security of the Ottoman state demanded, there were forced conversions. Every four years the most vigorous boys were taken from the towns and villages, willingly or not, to be trained as janissaries (a word from the Turkish *yeni cheri*, or new troops). Thus, even in the years of order, the Turkish conquest was a harsh experience.

Moreover, the Turkish overlordship created a Balkan mosaic of legal, social and economic relations. In Bosnia-Hercegovina and in Albania, there were wholesale conversions to Islam by nobility and peasantry alike. There, a largely homogeneous society evolved which continued the old social and economic hierarchy more or less intact. Those who had been chieftains and members of the landed nobility before the conquest continued as such thereafter.

In Bulgaria, Serbia and Macedonia, on the other hand, the old nobility had been swept away in the wars of conquest and a new nobility had been installed over the peasantry, an alien Turkish nobility. In these regions the old social distinctions were wiped out and a largely egalitarian peasant society emerged. In the Danubian Principalities, as Walachia and Moldavia in present-day Romania came to be known, the Turkish overlordship was again different. There, the local nobility was allowed to continue largely as before, as long as the sultan received his tribute and his local officials collected their bribes—or baksheesh.

ANTI-TURK HERO, the 15th Century Albanian chief Skanderbeg led a short-lived Balkan revolt against Ottoman rule.

In these regions under the Turkish dominion the lot of the peasantry deteriorated catastrophically—largely as a result of the tyranny and exactions inflicted by Christians on Christians. Worse still, in the Danubian Principalities a system grew up by which the local lords—the boyars—and the Greek civil servants of the Ottoman state could purchase titles and jurisdiction for a term of years, recouping their expenses by savage taxation of the luckless peasants. This practice of the sale of office and justice was widespread throughout the Empire, but in Romania it reached fantastic proportions

and left a legacy of cynicism and corruption which has begun to wane only recently.

Thus in each of the zones of Turkish conquest, the lot of the people varied. What was uniform to all was the experience of alien overlordship and the legacy of violence as the cohesion and power of the Empire declined. When the Empire passed its apex of power in the 17th and 18th Centuries, the conditions of the subject peoples took a catastrophic turn for the worse. All military discipline was lost. The central authority broke down. It was in these later years that the proverb came into vogue: "Where the Turk trod, no grass grows." Within the Empire, the 17th and 18th Century military officials, the beys and the *dahis*, savagely oppressed the people; they were scarcely to be distinguished from the robber bands, the omnipresent haiduks who lurked in the forests and mountain passes.

In border areas like Montenegro or in the pirate state of Senj on the Adriatic coast, brigandage became for centuries a hereditary way of life. There was an external threat to order as well, for as the Ottoman state declined, Austria and Russia pressed to the attack, moving into the vacuum created by the collapse of Turkish military power. On the frontiers, war —and with it the parallel evils of yearly murder, rape and arson—became as regular as the cycle of seasons. In the southwest, in the Dinaric highlands of Albania and Montenegro, peoples racially akin (although sundered by religion) raided back and forth across the fluid frontiers, casually inflicting atrocities on their enemies and, within their own societies, acknowledging little but the law of vendetta.

In central Macedonia, Serbia and the Sanjak, the situation was not much different. There the brigands took to the hills and forests, carrying on an outlaw life of rebellion against the central power—an existence of chronic violence that they rationalized as being at least better than that of the downtrodden peasantry around them.

Thus, in the years of the Ottoman decline, the effects on the Balkans were very largely negative. There were few positive effects, except for the formation of certain features of the Balkan character which have earned nearly universal admiration—pride in self, courage in war, contempt for the sufferings of flesh, an unbreakable sense of community and a generosity to friends.

The chief enemies of the Turks in the first years of the European counterattack were the Austrians and their allies. It would be many years before the Turks were a negligible force in battle—in 1683 they were again powerful enough to besiege Vienna—but under great military commanders like Ludwig of Baden and Eugene of Savoy, the Austrians liberated Hungary and Transylvania. Then, in a series of daring campaigns near the end of the century, they drove south as far as Bulgaria and Macedonia.

THE first Austrian offensive was repelled by the Ottomans. The subject peoples who had hailed the Austrians' coming were savagely punished; one consequence was a mass flight of Serbs to the populated lands north of the Danube, there to form the nucleus of the native Balkan liberation movement in later centuries. But the Austrian campaign was a sign of the future. More ominous still for the Turks was the fact that far to the northeast loomed the young giant, imperial Russia, then under the aegis of Peter the Great, who was bent on transforming his patrimony from a remote, backward, semi-Byzantine country into a modern European autocratic state.

Peter was ambitious for the Turkish legacy. There had been, even in medieval times, a strong quality of messianism in Russian political theories. The grand dukes of Moscow had frequently pictured themselves as the heirs of Byzantium and their capital as another Rome. What more natural consequence of these theories than that imperial Russia proclaim itself the champion of the Balkan Christian peoples, especially of the Russians' brother Slavs within the Turkish Empire? In the process, the Russians reasoned, they might also gain a long-desired strategic, warm-water outlet on the Bosporus and, in Montenegro, a window on the Adriatic as well.

THE first Russo-Turkish war dates from 1676-1681, when the armies of the two states collided in what is now the Soviet Crimea. By 1696 Peter had taken the Turkish holdings in Azov; he was eventually to proclaim himself publicly, and no doubt cynically, as the defender of Balkan Christendom, although it was some years before Russia could field the military power necessary to fulfill this grandiose ambition.

But Russian power grew steadily. Under Catherine the Great, Russia became a major factor in Balkan affairs. In 1782 Catherine proposed to the Austrians that they end their rivalry in the Balkans, and offered a dazzling plan: the western regions of the Balkans would fall to the Habsburgs in return for their support of a reborn Greek-Byzantine empire. The new empire was to be a Russian puppet under the rule of Catherine's grandson, who was christened Constantine in anticipation of the occasion.

Nothing came of this grandiose scheme, but the plan itself was merely one instance of the fancied opportunities of the great powers of Europe—Austria, Russia, Britain and France—in this primitive southeastern corner of the continent. What this habit of chronic intervention in Balkan affairs was to mean for the precarious diplomacy of the 19th Century, as the European powers competed for national advantage in the rotting legacy of the Grand Turk, was accurately and cynically put by Nicholas I, Czar of all the Russias, to the British ambassador in St. Petersburg. "We have on our hands a sick man, a very sick man," said Nicholas in 1853. "It will be a great misfortune if one of these days he should happen to slip away before the necessary arrangements were made."

The necessary arrangements were never made. The great powers tried to dispose of events, ordering the breakup of the Turkish holdings in Europe as suited their own imperial interests; but throughout the 19th Century there were other actors on the scene—passionate actors, turbulent, unruly, exacerbated by the ordeal of alien rule and the apparently imminent prospect of national liberation. They proceeded to take events into their own hands, and although few anticipated it, the result—for the great powers as much as anyone else—was ruin.

As the ideas of liberty proclaimed by philosophers and acted out by national armies convulsed Europe in the French Revolution and the subsequent Napoleonic Wars, new influences had disturbed the troubled sleep of the Balkans. Napoleon had humbled the old dynasties, remade the political map of Europe, and carried the idea of the free nation wherever he marched. In 1797 he had abolished the Venetian state and begun the organization of the Kingdom of Illyria. In the Balkans the new ideas began to take hold: what Western Europe could do, the subject Balkan peoples might do as well. The first scholars of the Balkan past, the first theorists of national revolution and the first military commanders of the modern type, as distinct from the old haiduk brigand-revolutionary, appear in the Balkans in the opening years of the 19th Century.

IN 1804 the Serbian highlanders, under the leadership of a rich peasant and pig-breeder, one Karageorge, rose against the forces of the local Turkish *dahis*. Initially proclaiming his rising a rebellion in *support* of the sultan, he quickly passed to the leadership of a national uprising on a heroic scale. Savage Turkish repression achieved little. At Niš in southeastern Serbia the Turks beheaded the troops of a local chieftain and built a tower of human skulls, but the rebellion dragged on.

Karageorge fled in 1813 to Austria, but in 1815 his rival, Miloš Obrenović, led a new revolt, one that this time succeeded. The repercussions of this victory were felt everywhere in the moribund Turkish Empire. The Greeks rebelled in 1821; by 1829 they had won effective independence. In that same year, the weakened Turks were forced to withdraw from the Danubian Principalities, which fell under the "protection" of Russia. The autonomy of Serbia was proclaimed in 1830. The sultan's flag still flew in Bucharest, Iaşi and Belgrade, but everyone knew the end was in sight.

FOR the Austrians and the Russians, these were the years of triumph. They felt a heady destiny. Both had once fought a desperate defensive battle against the Turks, and now both saw themselves as entering into the Turkish inheritance. But Russia was itself a backward and distraught nation, not usually impressive in offensive military operations except by comparison with the failing and demoralized Turks. The Austrians understood their political situation even less than the czars understood theirs. The Habsburg monarchy was a jerry-built structure, an uneasy, polyglot alliance of Christian peoples held together through the centuries by the danger of the Turk. As the Turkish threat waned, the cohesion of the Habsburg monarchy waned too. Few knew it. But sick as the "sick man of Europe" was, he would ironically outlive—by a few weeks at least—the two monarchies which sought to pilfer his estate.

Seventeen years before the outbreak of the world war which was finally to take the life of the sick man, Chancellor Otto von Bismarck of Germany grumbled that "some damned foolish thing in the Balkans" would touch off the conflagration. Bismarck was an accurate prophet, but there is little to suggest that he acted decisively to avert the impending tragedy. In concert with the other statesmen of his time, Bismarck sought to adjust differences among the great powers, but he did not essentially dissent from the idea of war. "The great problems of our time will not be resolved by speeches and majority decisions," he once said, "but by blood and iron." In the Balkans, Europe was to find blood enough to satisfy even the Iron Chancellor.

The chronicle of 19th Century rivalries in the Balkans is a complex one. There are the conflicting ambitions of the great powers which came to a head again and again, as in the Crimean War when Britain and France joined with Turkey to counter an ambitious Russian intervention in the Danubian Principalities and Austria played the role of a self-seeking neutral. The European powers clashed again after the Bosnian and Bulgarian uprising of 1875-1878, when Austria was permitted to proclaim a "protectorate" over Bosnia-Hercegovina. When Russia set up a new Bulgarian puppet state after a Russo-Turkish war in 1877, the powers intervened in concert to alter the map, reducing the new Bulgarian state to a shadow of itself.

There were also the rivalries of the emergent Balkan states themselves which, viewing the cynical diplomacies of the great powers, managed even to exceed their teachers' cynicism and malevolence. In 1885, when the population of Rumelia, as southern Bulgaria was then called, rose in rebellion against the sultan, the Serbian armies launched an attack on the northern Bulgars who had marched to the aid of their compatriots. The result in this case was a military disaster for the Serbs. But the Bulgars could not claim unalloyed virtue; achieving independence, they denied full freedom to the national minorities in their own midst.

NO rational political map could be drawn in the Balkans, and no one in the Balkans, it seemed, cared for rational politics in any case. The ancient empires of Simeon, Stefan Dušan, Michael the Brave and John Zápolya crowded each other on the map, and Balkan peoples yearned to re-create them all. The passionate national ambitions of the small Balkan lands, each proclaiming a messianic destiny grotesque enough in the case of larger nations like Austria and Russia, could not possibly be fulfilled. Yet each of these peoples was prepared to try, and no brutality in support of policy was unthinkable, no price was too great to pay.

The alliances and coalitions among the Balkan states, and among the "protecting" great powers, formed, dissolved and formed again with bewildering speed. In the First Balkan War in 1912, for example, the Serbs, Greeks, Bulgars and Montenegrins cooperated briefly against the common enemy, the Turk. Yet within a few weeks of the armistice war broke out again—this time producing a new coalition as Serbs, Montenegrins, Greeks and Romanians teamed up *with* the Turks to despoil an intransigent Bulgaria of its gains.

It was a situation which could not go on, could not endure, and it did not. On June 28, 1914—on the 525th anniversary of the tragedy of Kosovo—the whole terrible issue came to a head as a Serbian nationalist, one Gavrilo Princip, assassinated the heir-presumptive to the Austrian throne and destroyed the precarious structure of Balkan—and world—peace.

ONCE again the story is replete with pathos. The Archduke Franz Ferdinand, the victim, was a curious and enigmatic figure—aloof, imperious, bourgeois in taste and habits, but something of a political pragmatist who understood that the entire structure of the Austro-Hungarian state would have to be remade if the Empire was to endure. Within that Empire two imperial peoples, the Germans and the Magyars (Hungarians), ruled over some few of intermediate status like the Poles of Galicia, and a larger mass of subject peoples—the Croats, Romanians, Czechs, Slovaks, Serbs and Slovenes. The arrogance and caprice of the Germans and Hungarians provoked the rising fury of the subject peoples, but Franz Ferdinand proposed to remake the Empire into a multinational confederation.

It was a laudable aim, but perhaps an impossible one. In any event, a revitalized Empire was a deadly threat to the national ambitions of the states surrounding the Austro-Hungarian monarchy. If the ambitions of the lesser peoples in the Empire could be satisfied, then Serbia, for example, would never manage to unite the "Yugoslavs," as the southern Slavic peoples were beginning to be known. The Serbian ambition was to lead a coalition of

Serbians, Montenegrins, Bosnians, Macedonians, Croats and Slovenes. To accomplish this end was state policy in Belgrade, the Serbian capital. Even more dangerously, it was the policy of semiofficial extremist and terrorist organizations like *Ujedinjenje ili Smrt* (Union or Death), a group which was under the direction of the mysterious Dragutin Dimitrijević, chief of Serbian Army Intelligence.

Known as Apis, Dimitrijević appears repeatedly in the tragedy of the assassination as the patron of Gavrilo Princip and his band. But the truth of his complicity will never fully be known. In Salonika, in 1917, in the course of the conflict which was at least partly his making, Dimitrijević was tried and executed in mysterious circumstances, taking his testimony to the grave.

Whatever the extent of the Serbian involvement in the assassination, the result was an assurance of unqualified support to the Austrians by the Germans and an Austrian ultimatum to the Serbians—so rudely couched as to raise the suspicion that it was designed to be rejected. The Serbians accepted most of the demands, but temporized on others. Whereupon Austria-Hungary, seeing its opportunity to destroy Serbia and prop up its failing hegemony in the Balkans, declared war. The rest of the story is world history: Russia threatened war, Germany backed the Austrians, the French honored their commitment to the Russians, the British honored their commitment to the French. The First World War came, a holocaust in which more than 8.5 million soldiers died and countless millions more were wounded, a tragedy which has changed the whole political course of the modern world.

TWO TANGLED BALKAN WARS

The two wars fought in the Balkans in 1912-1913 prefigured World War I; when the larger conflict broke out, all the Balkan nations found themselves fighting the same enemies they had just warred with. The First Balkan War began on October 8, 1912, when Montenegro declared war on Turkey. It was joined by Bulgaria, Serbia and Greece, all eager to seize the Turks' remaining European territories. Turkey was defeated, but the allies instantly quarreled. The Serbs demanded Salonika and a larger share of Macedonia from Bulgaria; the Greeks made similar demands. On June 29, 1913, Bulgaria attacked Serbia and Greece. Montenegro, Romania and Turkey joined the Serbs and Greeks, and Bulgaria was defeated. In World War I, the Serbians, Montenegrins, Romanians and Greeks joined the Allies. Their late enemy, Bulgaria, joined the Central Powers along with Turkey.

What concerns us here is something less: the effects on the Balkan lands which were merely in 1914 the unfortunate pivot of world history. Poor, distracted, the prey of the great powers and the prey, too, of pathological domestic politics, they had been exhausted by the preceding Balkan wars and many of their leaders, with the exception of those of Serbia and Montenegro, pitiably sought to avoid being sucked into the world maelstrom. They could not remain neutral long. For them, World War I loosed a renewed orgy of destruction. Their losses were proportionately enormous. Out of a population of three million, Serbia alone lost 757,000 civilians and soldiers. In 1915 the Serbian armies, after initial successes, were driven out of their homeland, retreating in an epic march with their women and children over snowy wastes to Albania, where they were evacuated to the island of Corfu by Allied ships. There the Serbians regrouped and returned to the attack less than a year later on the bloody Salonika front.

Nor would the story of Balkan tragedy end with World War I. When in 1918 peace returned to the world, it did not return to the Balkans. The Austro-Hungarian monarchy was in ruins, the empires of the czars and sultans had collapsed, Bulgaria had been defeated and Serbia and Montenegro were exhausted by the bloodletting. Nothing was truly won in this war. Romania and Serbia gained new territories but inherited new political and social problems with them. Thus all the warring contenders can be said to have lost. No political settlement that could be expected to endure emerged after the holocaust. The old ambitions still burned. The old hatreds were, if anything, more intense.

While a few men sit in a café in Krujë and a boy studies a poster, a woman in Moslem peasant costume passes by. Albanian women

An Isolated Corner with a Bleak History and Dark Prospects

Although the Ottoman Empire has long since vanished, its influence continues in one corner of the Balkans. Most Albanians are Moslems, and they also endure the bad conditions which existed under their former Turkish rulers. With its widespread illiteracy and poverty, Albania seems out of another age. But entering its borders is as much a leap into the future

do much of the manual labor while the men frequent cafés.

as a descent into the past. No other country so closely foreshadows the tyrannical, stifling society imagined by George Orwell in his novel *1984*. Concentration camps full of political prisoners, hordes of spies and informers, censored radio and books, and restricted travel are aspects of Albanian life that come close to fulfilling the grimmest of Orwell's predictions.

LAVDI PUNONJESVE TE DALLUAR

WORKER HEROES who have set an example on their jobs have their photographs displayed in Tirana. Like other Communist nations, Albania encourages group projects by praising successful individuals.

SEASIDE RESORT of Durrës draws Albanians to the beach on a summer day *(opposite)*. Fearing desertions, the police strictly control all boating and even swimming.

STATUE OF STALIN guards Liberation Square in Tirana *(right)*. The only Communist countries that have not recently denounced Stalin's excesses are China and Albania.

DESOLATE AVENUE with its lonely traffic policeman *(below)* symbolizes Albania's frustrated pride. Tirana has broad boulevards, but few of its citizens can afford cars.

A GENTLER ECHO *of the past is found in the folk customs of Romanian peasants*

VILLAGE COUPLES in Cluj, Transylvania, gather on a balcony to watch the dancing at a celebration. The peasants build their own homes and take great pride in their craftsmanship.

EXUBERANT DANCING on a Sunday afternoon attracts children in native Romanian costume. Such tunics date from the Roman Empire and adorn a frieze on Trajan's Column in Rome.

PEASANT GIRLS walk across a field to witness the Sunday festivities. The details of design in a peasant woman's clothing can reveal to an expert what region she comes from.

ELEGANT EMBROIDERY adorns the vests and blouses of two Magyar girls *(below)* in Cluj. Although it is now part of Romania, Transylvania in earlier times belonged to Hungary.

Operating from secret headquarters on the island of Vis, Marshal Tito (right) plans his 1944 campaign against the Germans. Next to

4

Years of Instability and Betrayal

IN November 1918, peace returned to the world, but in the Balkans it was a fitful peace. Perhaps it can hardly be termed a peace so much as a twilight state of chronic civil violence and instability, scarcely to be distinguished from war.

The great empires of Austria-Hungary, Russia and Turkey—empires which had for centuries determined the destiny of the Balkans —had foundered. The Fourteen Points propounded by President Woodrow Wilson of the United States held out the promise of national self-determination and freedom for the Balkan nations, to be sure. But how was the naïve optimism of the United States, that happy and guarded enclave of 18th Century rationalism, to be squared with the tragic realities of the Balkan historical experience? How were the passionate and conflicting ambitions of these nations to be gratified? How could the wrongs inflicted by the defeated states be expunged? How could the psychological wounds resulting from years of carnage and destruction be healed?

Compounding such questions were the still unsolved riddles of the Balkan past. In each nation, in addition to the ravages left by the war itself, there survived the atrocities and miseries of 500 years of alien rule: internal social cleavages, poverty, squalor, ignorance, obscurantism and nationalist mysticism.

THE war, in addition, left a taste in the Balkans for political excess and betrayal on a scale hardly ever before contemplated, even in so tragedy-ridden a land. Of the four Balkan nations, one had taken its place among the new states in 1918—but its very existence was denied by its neighbors. This was Albania, a state whose freedom had technically been proclaimed in 1912, but whose national existence before the war was sketchy in the extreme. Another Balkan power seemed—but only seemed —to be blessed by the outcome of the war. The unified Kingdom of the Serbs, Croats and Slovenes—later to be renamed Yugoslavia, "the Land of the South Slavs"—emerged out of old Serbia, Montenegro, Bosnia-Hercegovina, Croatia, Dalmatia, Slovenia and a large part of Macedonia. The new kingdom exceeded the most grandiose dreams of the old pan-Serb plotters. Yet rancor quickly developed in the new state between the Roman Catholic Croats now freed of Habsburg rule and the Orthodox Serbians who regarded themselves as the historic nucleus, and thus the natural leaders, of the new state.

Romania also seemed to have gained by the war. To the old principalities of Walachia and Moldavia were now added the province of Transylvania and the territory of Bukovina, awarded as war booty at the expense of defeated Austria-Hungary. Romania also acquired the northeastern province of Bessarabia, an area which the newborn Soviet Union, rent by civil war, was not powerful enough to retain.

The war, on the other hand, left defeated Bulgaria dazed and incredulous—angry, frustrated and bitter at the realization that the bloodlettings and sacrifice of three national wars in the space of six years had left the nation poorer and yet farther from achieving its national ambitions than when the ill-considered adventures had begun. Political discontent smoldered, and the nation, although ethnically homogeneous, was brutally divided internally along ideological lines.

Extremist movements sprang up: on the Right, there was the proto-Fascist Internal Macedonian Revolutionary Organization (IMRO), which demanded the annexation of Greek and Yugoslav Macedonia. On the Left, there were the Agrarians, led by Alexander Stambuliski. Stambuliski was a farseeing, strong-willed politician who as Premier of Bulgaria instituted social reforms, accelerated the spread of education to the mountain villages, built roads and sought a reconciliation with Yugoslavia —a policy which was to lead to his downfall. The Bulgarian Communists briefly cooperated with Stambuliski, but took no action when his Government was overthrown in 1923 by a reactionary coup d'état amid scenes of unspeakable brutality. Stambuliski was tortured and made to dig his own grave. His right arm —"the arm and the hand that signed the Treaty of Niš," which had attempted to curb IMRO terrorism on the Yugoslav frontier—was severed from his body. Then he was beheaded.

ATROCITY engendered atrocity. Bulgarian political parties made a practice of murder. The IMRO carried on a program of wholesale assassination against its opponents—those who counseled a policy of reconciliation with neighboring countries and even those in its own moderate wing who sought to establish an autonomous status for Macedonia rather than to annex it. The Communists followed similar tactics; in April 1925, the Party organized what may have been the single most ambitious assassination attempt in Balkan history when it narrowly missed killing King Boris but succeeded in assassinating a prominent member of the Bulgarian Parliament, General Kosta Georgiev, on the 14th of the month. Two days later, the Party dynamited the Svyata Nedelja

Cathedral in Sofia during Georgiev's funeral services, killing 128 persons and wounding hundreds of others.

Such episodes were anything but rare in the postwar Balkans. In 1928, a half-crazed Montenegrin deputy shot six deputies in the Yugoslav Parliament, killing two on the spot. Stepan Radić, leader of the Croatian opposition, was wounded and died a few weeks later. The Croats gave as good as they got. In 1934, the Ustasha, a Croatian hypernationalist, Fascist and terrorist organization, joined forces with the Bulgarian IMRO and murdered King Alexander of Yugoslavia.

In 1938, King Carol of Romania, fighting to maintain his royal dictatorship against the challenge of Corneliu Codreanu, leader of the "Legion of the Archangel Michael," or, as it came to be known, the Romanian "Iron Guard," ordered the murder of Codreanu and 13 others "while attempting to escape." Codreanu himself had come to national attention in 1924 for the assassination of the police chief of Iași, and again in 1933, when he murdered the then Romanian Premier, Ion Duca. Truly, in the Balkan lands, terror was banal.

The turmoil is understandable. The Balkan states were hopelessly trapped. In the prewar years, the naïve dream of the nationalist agitators had been that social justice and civil peace would come automatically as liberation was achieved and foreign oppression ended— according to vaguely apprehended but devoutly believed laws of history. Yet the Balkan states between 1918 and 1939 merely prefigured the postcolonial agony of our own time: they

were playing out the drama we have seen again and again in postwar Indonesia, Ghana and the Congo, to name only three cases at the center of the contemporary world stage.

Then, as now, foreign oppression ended only to be succeeded by new political despotisms. Societies long slumbering and devoid of the skills demanded by a modern industrial age engendered, on the Right and on the Left, political movements barren of real political understanding, impatient of reason, and exalting quasi-mystical solutions (Marxist and anti-Marxist) that were as grandiose as they were vague.

The problems that were to confront the Balkan nations in the interwar years were infinitely more complex than the national preoccupations of preceding decades. One phase of the national liberation struggle ended with the expulsion of the Turks and the Austrians. But what could be the simple solution to the age-old problems of illiteracy, undercapitalization, technological incompetence, and racial and religious prejudice which afflicted the region? The Balkans, although they were part of the continent of Europe, were not part of the advanced technological culture of the West. Agriculture in these regions remained primitive—peasants still worked their fields with a wooden plow not very different from one described by Vergil in his *Georgics* some 2,000 years ago. Everywhere in the Balkans, more than half the population lived on the land or derived its livelihood from it: about 75 per cent of 18 million Romanians, roughly 80 per cent of seven million Bulgarians, 75 per cent of 16 million Yugoslavs and

ROMANIA'S FANATICAL IRON GUARD

Of all the terrorist groups which plagued Balkan politics in the years between the wars, none was more wildly fanatical than the Romanian "Legion of the Archangel Michael," which came to be known as the Iron Guard. From its founding in the 1920s to the late 1930s, it was responsible for uncounted political assassinations. Fascist, rabidly anti-Semitic and passionately nationalistic, the Guard held its meetings at midnight in forest glades, with members wearing tiny bags filled with "the sacred Romanian soil" around their necks. Like Adolf Hitler's followers, Guard members favored colored shirts (green, in their case), special war cries ("All for the Fatherland!") and sweeping salutes. More than one Romanian regime attempted to destroy the Guard, but with little success. It enjoyed widespread support, winning 16 per cent of the vote in the 1937 Romanian elections. The Guard was dealt a shattering blow in 1938, however, when King Carol, who was establishing a royalist dictatorship of his own, ordered the killing of 14 of its top leaders. It had been by far the most successful Fascist movement in the Balkans.

some 90 per cent of one million Albanians.

The landholding system was not uniform throughout the area. In Bulgaria and Yugoslavia (particularly in the southeastern regions) the farm holdings were fairly evenly distributed. Fewer than 17 per cent of the Bulgarian peasants, for example, owned farms larger than 25 acres. But in Romania, a truly "feudal" land system had prevailed up to the end of World War I (a peasant rising in 1907 had been savagely repressed). There, and in southern Albania, much agrarian discontent festered.

EVEN where land had been redistributed, other problems remained. There were tens of thousands of "dwarf holders" in the Balkans; the pressures on the land were enormous. The small farmsteads were called upon to support families of a dozen or more, all living together in crowded squalor. The peasant had little cash for fertilizers or machine equipment, and he was nearly always at the mercy of the world commodity market. He sold his produce at depressed prices and bought his manufactured goods at high ones. This was the notorious Balkan "price-scissors" that gave rise to so much peasant political agitation in the years between the wars.

In the cities, conditions were sometimes hardly better, although a nascent industry and a middle class were beginning to emerge. Most unsettling was the development of an unemployed—and often unemployable—intelligentsia. The cafés of Belgrade, Zagreb, Sofia and Bucharest were crowded with journalists and lawyers who were tinder for any extremist political movement. From their ranks were recruited the cadres of the future Communist and Fascist Parties alike.

These men, and the movements they staffed, along with the peasants who sank each year into what seemed a more hopeless and unjust degradation, fell easy prey to ambitious politicians and ideologies. They were prey to the machinations of foreign powers as well.

The old Habsburg and Romanov monarchies had been toppled, and with them the old dynastic ambitions of Austria-Hungary and imperial Russia. But as World War I receded in time, the Balkans once again became the arena of great power rivalries. This time a chief actor was Italy, which coveted Yugoslavia's Adriatic coast and, to bring pressure on the Yugoslavs, therefore encouraged Bulgarian nationalist ambitions as well as any promising internal separatist movement within Albania and Yugoslavia.

Italy, if only indirectly, was implicated in the assassination of Yugoslavia's King Alexander in 1934; more productive of long-term results were Mussolini's steady encroachments into Albania. There, after a brief flirtation with democratic institutions in the immediate postwar years, under the leadership of an Orthodox bishop-turned-politician, Fan Noli, the nation fell under the dictatorship of an ambitious tribal chieftain, one Ahmed Bey Zogu (later King Zog I), whose chronic economic difficulties increasingly forced him to accept eagerly proffered Italian financial credit. Albania became virtually an Italian puppet, but Italian influence elsewhere in the Balkans was to fade as Italian strength proved inadequate to Mussolini's dream of a revived Roman Empire. The real actors on the Balkan scene in the 1930s eventually turned out to be Adolf Hitler and Josef Stalin.

SOVIET influence was clandestine. For most of the interwar period, the Balkan Communist Parties were outlawed, and local Communists were driven into exile. The cadres of the future Balkan Communist Parties were nevertheless forming underground; among their ranks was an obscure organizer named Josip Broz, known as Tito. A Croatian machinist, he had served in the Austro-Hungarian Army during World War I and been taken prisoner by the Russians. After the Russian Revolution, he had been thoroughly trained in Communist subversive tactics. In 1937, Tito became the chief of the Yugoslav Communist movement and began organizing the underground communications network that was to serve him well in the wartime struggle a few years later.

Nazi political warfare was by contrast overt. The Nazis used both economic weapons and propaganda, but there were normal diplomatic operations as well. In 1940 Romania joined the Berlin-Rome Axis; in 1941 Bulgaria followed suit. By 1939 Albania had surrendered even the pretense of independence as Mussolini sent in troops and consolidated his grip on the country. King Zog was forced to flee into exile.

THE instability of Balkan politics in the interwar years was, for all the melodramatic violence, only part of a larger European malaise. In a sense, all Europe had become Balkanized after 1918 as men awoke from the ordeal of the trenches to find that they had created a world in which simple justice was not being done. When World War II finally came in the autumn of 1939, it was not, for once, a spark in the Balkans that ignited the conflagration. The immediate causes of that war lay to the north, in Poland. But Poland was not far away, and the Balkans, as a primary zone of conflict between Hitler's Germany and the new eastern colossus, the Soviet Union, could not hope to remain out of the war for long.

The cynical Nazi-Soviet Pact of 1939, which temporarily freed Hitler from concern over Russia and enabled him to pursue his war against Poland and the Western democracies, constituted an abortive effort to narrow the area of conflict by defining German and Soviet spheres of influence. Secret sections of the pact called attention to Soviet interests in Bessarabia, while Germany expressed disinterest in the region. But the alliance between thieves could not last. Apart from the eastern half of Poland, torn from the Polish corpse after the Nazi armies had conquered the country, the Soviets demanded the Romanian-held regions of Bessarabia and northern Bukovina. Here for the first time the Nazis and the Soviets came into serious conflict. The Russians had not previously indicated that they wanted Bukovina. To avoid trouble, the Nazis gave way, but Hitler did not forget the double-dealing.

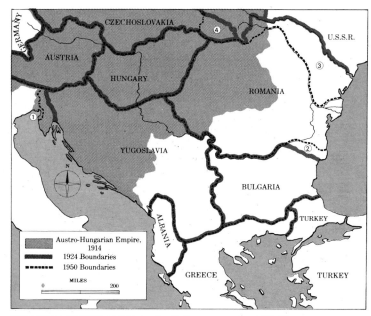

SHIFTING BOUNDARIES in the Balkan area since World War I are outlined above. Before World War I, much of the region belonged to the Austro-Hungarian Empire, whose collapse in 1918 led to the emergence of Yugoslavia and the enlargement of Romania. After World War II, four territorial changes took place in the area. Italy's province of Venezia Giulia (1), which included the Istrian peninsula, was ceded to Yugoslavia. Southern Dobrudja (2), which Bulgaria had lost to Romania in 1913, was restored to Bulgaria. Bessarabia (3), which had been taken over by Romania after World War I, was returned to the U.S.S.R. North of Romania, the former Czechoslovakian area of Carpatho-Ukraine (4), which had been annexed by Hungary in 1938 and 1939, was taken over by Russia.

The Russians, moreover, were by no means satisfied. In November 1940, Vyacheslav M. Molotov, the Soviet Foreign Minister, was in Germany demanding more—in particular, a new Soviet sphere of influence in Bulgaria and access to the Dardanelles. But Hitler himself had a growing interest in southeastern Europe. The Greeks, attacked some weeks earlier by Mussolini's troops, had flung the Italian armies back into Albania; the Germans feared that the British would intervene in support of the Greeks, opening a new front on the continent. Romania and Bulgaria formed a vital logistic lifeline for any German attack overland against Greece. So too did Yugoslavia. To consolidate the German flank in the Balkans, the Nazi Foreign Office sought to force Yugoslavia, too, into the Axis.

Yugoslavia, now ruled by the inept regent Prince Paul, cousin of the assassinated King

Alexander, had traditionally pursued a pro-French and pro-British diplomacy. But Paul was intimidated by German might. On March 25, 1941, he sent emissaries to Vienna to sign a treaty of alliance with Germany. The result was a coup d'état led by patriotic Army elements. Paul was overthrown. King Peter, Alexander's young son, was installed in his place as Chief of State, and delirious crowds surged through the streets of Belgrade, cheering the news of the coup, denouncing the Nazis and boldly proclaiming *"Bolje rat nego pakt"*—"Better war than the pact." Yugoslavia, as Prime Minister Winston Churchill was to put it, "had found its soul"—if, indeed, it had ever lost it.

The price was blood. For nearly two years the Balkans had avoided the terrors of war. Now the war was to come with a terrible vengeance. Shocked by Yugoslavia's display of independence and spirit, Hitler reacted in a rage. On April 6, 1941, the Nazi armies struck across the Yugoslav frontiers, invading simultaneously from Germany, Hungary, Romania and Bulgaria.

ALL organized resistance collapsed in little more than a week. The German armies crashed through to the Adriatic and the Aegean, rolled up the flank of the Greek forces in Albania and, in the world's first great airborne invasion, went on to seize Crete from the British. The campaign was a total military success. But the Yugoslav adventure was to cost Hitler dear.

The Balkan campaign, for one thing, had delayed the launching of *Barbarossa*—the great attack on the Soviet Union which Hitler had ordered in December 1940, as it finally became clear that Nazi and Soviet ambitions were incompatible. This delay of a few weeks was a factor in bringing the Nazi attack to a halt in the winter snows of Russia only a few miles from Moscow.

The delay was a basic Nazi miscalculation. Another mistake would cost Hitler equally dear. The Führer had forgotten the fundamental lesson of the Balkan past: there was a law

of nemesis operative in the Balkans. Interventions by great powers invited retribution, as Austria-Hungary had once learned. Organized military resistance might be crushed in the Balkan mountains, but to stamp out the old brigand tradition was something entirely different. Yugoslavia might be dismembered, but a bloody guerrilla war would go on.

ALL this, however, lay in the future. In 1941 Yugoslavia was prostrate and broken. The Nazis hastened to reward their Balkan allies at Yugoslavia's expense. Germany itself seized northern Slovenia. Italy occupied Montenegro and took southern Slovenia and a large part of Dalmatia. Bulgaria was allotted Macedonia and frontier districts of southeastern Serbia; Hungary seized areas in northern Yugoslavia. Croatia was reconstituted as a nominal kingdom, under an Italian princeling who wisely refrained from visiting his new possession. Actual power in Croatia was wielded by Ante Pavelić, a psychotic Ustasha leader who proceeded to murder tens of thousands of Serbians and Jews. Serbia itself, once the core of the Yugoslav state, was made into a German puppet. Yugoslavia had been expunged from the map.

Almost from the beginning there was resistance. It started, as might have been predicted, in central Serbia, the heartland of the old haiduk tradition, where shattered remnants of the Royal Yugoslav Army took to the woods after their defeat by the Germans. These were the Chetniks. Later, after the Nazi armies had launched their attack on the Soviet Union in June 1941, Communist-led forces also took the field. They were to become known in history as the Partisans.

The true history of the war in the Balkans can never be known. There is a welter of conflicting testimony; passions were too hotly engaged; much evidence has been falsified. But the fundamental guide to understanding is that the tragic story of guerrilla resistance in Yugoslavia is a Balkan story, an incomprehensible episode when viewed by Westerners unfamiliar with the Balkan tangle. The guerrilla war in

Yugoslavia was as much a multisided civil war as a resistance. The contending forces battled for political supremacy and engaged in bloody reprisals as much as they fought against Germans and Italians. Nevertheless, for all the passions engaged, the outlines of something approaching the truth are knowable.

Under their leader, Draža Mihailović, a former colonel on the Yugoslav General Staff, the Chetniks were among the first to take up arms against the Nazis. They suffered, however, from fatal defects. First, they were primarily a Serbian movement and they could not make an appeal to larger national and political ideals. The Chetniks feared, secondly, that if Serbians were to bear disproportionate losses in World War II as they had in World War I, when the Serbians lost some 757,000 soldiers and civilians, the Serbian position in postwar Yugoslavia would be fatally compromised. They were consequently somewhat more vulnerable to intimidation by reprisal. Finally, they were essentially a premodern movement—a haiduk campaign—with little understanding of the modern requirements of political programs and central direction.

The Partisans suffered from none of these disabilities. Their goals were utopian and supranational: all of Yugoslavia's prewar ills, economic and social, would disappear as power passed at last to the people. As a national movement, the Partisans were able to operate throughout Yugoslavia, skillfully evading identification with regional ambitions. And as militant Communists, they made good use of the knowledge of organization and covert communication which long experience in underground operations, as members of an illegal political movement, had taught them.

BEYOND that, the Partisans, whatever their faults and limitations, had true *élan:* they believed that they were the wave of the future and that the Chetniks were merely conservators of a dying past. As the war progressed, Partisan morale would grow. The Partisan forces were hardened by battle—hardened even by

repeated defeat. But the Chetniks, after the first savage reprisals by the Germans against the population of Serbia, lapsed into immobility in accordance with Mihailović's belief that large-scale resistance was unwise in the face of so formidable an enemy.

In all fairness, it must be said that the Chetniks did not concede the issue easily. The war in the Balkans and the war in the West were scarcely related experiences. Although the Nazis inflicted dreadful horrors on the Danes, Norwegians, French, Belgians and Dutch, they were even more brutal in the East. At Kragujevats in central Serbia, in a crime against civilians which is still virtually unknown to the outside world, German soldiers in a single day machine-gunned 8,000 people into a common grave on the outskirts of town; whole classes of high-school students marched out with their teachers to die. It is no wonder that the Chetniks were intimidated. They were afraid, as well, of the ultimate Communist conquest that loomed in the future—more so, it appears, than of the Nazis. So great was the Chetnik antipathy to Tito's coming to power that by the war's end, some of Mihailović's local commanders had become guilty of collaboration with the occupation forces—and even with the hated Ustasha.

BY 1944 the British had withdrawn all but token support from the Chetnik forces. The Yugoslav Government-in-Exile in London, which earlier in the war had proclaimed Mihailović its Minister of War, was forced by the Western Allies into an uneasy coalition with the Partisans. After all, the Partisans had at times tied down as many as 15 German divisions, and the British, at least, had not yet given up all hope of influencing them. The British hope was to prove idle, however; the Partisan leaders, as disciplined Communists, owed their loyalty to Moscow (although Moscow had helped them little enough).

As the sober testimony of high-ranking Partisans like Milovan Djilas and Vladimir Dedijer has made clear since the war, Partisan leaders could not conceive in those years of a clash of interest between the Soviet Union, "the Fatherland of Socialism," and their own national aspirations. Only time would teach them otherwise. On the island of Vis, to which he had been evacuated by the British after a German surprise attack in 1944, Tito evaded British efforts to conclude a political understanding. In late September he left the island for Moscow to coordinate plans with the Soviet leaders, whose armies were then approaching the Yugoslav frontiers.

E LSEWHERE the story of Communist intransigence and double-dealing was essentially the same. In Albania, as in Yugoslavia, resistance to the Italians and Germans polarized around Left and Right. There the forces of the Left (the *Lëvizje Nacionalçlirimtarë*, or National Liberation Movement) were led by the embryonic Communist Party, organized under the tutelage of the Yugoslav Communists. There were two Right-Wing groups which challenged the Communist claim to resistance leadership—the *Ballë Kombëtare* and the *Legalitete*. The Communists carried on savage warfare against the *Ballë Kombëtare* forces, succeeded in painting them as collaborators, and eventually destroyed them. The *Legalitete* forces served under Abas Kupi, a conservative tribal chieftain loyal to King Zog but a steadfast opponent of the Italians and Germans. His forces made a vigorous fight throughout the war without the slightest taint of collaboration.

Abas Kupi was, however, no more politically adept than Mihailović. The thrust and counterthrust of diplomacy, intrigue, blackmail and threat were beyond him. Like Mihailović, he was essentially backward-looking, mired in the past rather than guided, like his Communist enemies, by a political vision—however brutal and mistaken as that vision would prove to be. Thus Enver Hoxha, the Albanian schoolteacher turned Communist-revolutionary, won the battle for foreign recognition, although his National Liberation Movement members soon demonstrated where their true sympathies lay

by threatening British liaison personnel. A year after the war's end, they had behaved so offensively—they even fired upon British warships off the Albanian coast—that the U.S. and Britain broke off diplomatic relations. By that time it was too late to matter. Albania was firmly wedded to the Soviet bloc—or rather, to put the case more accurately, it had become a Yugoslav puppet, a satellite's satellite.

In Romania and Bulgaria the diplomatic and internal political situation (and consequently, the problem facing the Communist Parties) was fundamentally different. Both countries, willingly or not, had joined in the war against the Allies and were guilty of war crimes. Bulgaria, faithful to its ancient political sentiments, had declared war on Britain and on the United States but had refused to declare war on the Soviet Union. The U.S.S.R. was regarded by the population at large as the successor to the 19th Century Russia which had supported the independence of Bulgaria, albeit as a buffer state between it and Austria-Hungary and the Ottoman Empire. Bulgaria must also be credited with another act of conscience, remarkable in an Axis puppet. Throughout the war the Bulgarian people tried to protect the Jews from the Nazis. But non-Slav Romania, which had lost northern Bukovina and Bessarabia to the Soviets, was not an admirer of Russia. On June 21, 1941, Romania declared war on the Soviet Union, and Romanian troops crossed the Soviet frontiers the following day, participating —gladly—in Hitler's Eastern campaign.

B Y all accounts the Romanian military record on the Eastern Front was surprisingly good. Some 30 Romanian divisions rapidly overran the southern Ukraine, conquering the region between the Bug and Dniester as far as Odessa on the Black Sea. Romania, by this time under the dictatorship of a venal Fascist general, Ion Antonescu, was awarded the entire region as compensation for its loss of northern Transylvania to Hungary and of southern Dobrudja to Bulgaria, the Nazis' other allies. Bessarabia and northern Bukovina were thus restored once again to the control of Romania.

But by far the greatest Romanian contribution to Hitler's cause was oil. In 1941 alone, Romania supplied Germany with 2.1 million tons of oil. A consequence was that Hitler's Panzer divisions were able to roll, and the Allies in retaliation repeatedly and savagely bombed Romania's oil fields. In August 1943, in the first great American air attack of the war, 178 B-24 Liberators attacked Ploesti and its refineries. Ninety Liberators failed to return to base. But the bombers came again and again.

By 1944, however, the tide had clearly turned against the Axis. Romania itself was exhausted by a military effort beyond its capabilities. In March 1944, the Romanians opened peace talks with the British and Americans in Cairo, clearly hoping for an intervention by the Western Allies to forestall a Soviet occupation of their country. The Allies, however, were faithful to their commitments to the Soviet Union. The Soviets were fully informed of the progress of negotiations. On April 2, 1944, Molotov implied in a public announcement that the U.S.S.R. would demand Bessarabia and Bukovina—the territories Stalin had acquired in 1940.

THE Soviet armies soon crossed the Romanian frontiers. With the armies came the political commissars and the "Muscovite Band" of prewar Romanian Communists who had fled persecution to the U.S.S.R. In August 1944, the young Romanian King Michael arrested the pro-Fascist Premier Antonescu and announced that Romania had accepted the Allied surrender terms. He also announced the formation of a government of "national union"—one in which liberal "bourgeois" leaders, men untainted by wartime collaboration, and Communists alike would serve. But the Soviets delayed the signing of a final armistice until September 12, 1944, by which time they had occupied all of Romania, including a number of zones it had been understood they would not enter. Thus the real power to dictate the Romanian peace lay with the Soviets.

Clearly, the Russians were playing a canny game.

How canny became even clearer in the Bulgarian case. George Kennan has justly observed that Soviet postwar aims were finite: Stalin, he concludes, wished essentially to regain those regions of Eastern and Central Europe which he had won in 1940, with Hitler's acquiescence, together with those regions he had been denied when the unstable Soviet-German understanding broke down in the spring of 1941. This is probably true. But the Soviets, under the cynical leadership of Stalin and Molotov, would play for much or little, and take what they could get.

IN August 1944, one week after the Romanian surrender, Bulgarian envoys opened talks in Cairo with Britain and the U.S., the only two major powers with which they were technically at war. The neutral Soviets were duly informed by the Western Allies, although, since Bulgaria had never declared war on the Soviet Union and the Soviet Union had never declared war on Bulgaria, the Soviet Government was not directly concerned. Stalin reacted with characteristic perfidy. On September 5, two days after the formation of a pro-Western Government in Bulgaria, he declared war, and quickly overran the country. The final armistice was signed in Moscow, and the Soviets thus served notice on the West that Bulgaria remained within their sphere.

Consequently, as 1944 ended, all the Balkans, with the exception of Greece, lay under occupation by Soviet armies or, at the very least, in Albania and large tracts of Yugoslavia, under the control of the armies of Soviet supporters.

Everywhere, as the new peace dawned, the prospect for the Balkan nations was once again gloomy. The brief interlude of freedom of the interwar years had ended in the horrors of World War II. The Fascist Governments and Axis military occupations were destroyed; for the Balkans, predictably, there was no relief from suffering, no real peace, no luck.

One nightmare had ended; now another would begin.

UNSUSPECTING PREY, King Alexander Obrenović and Queen Draga of Serbia are shown a few days before their assassination by Army officers in June 1903. The mustachioed officer just to the left of the man in the derby is Dragutin Dimitrijević, who directed the plot and later helped plan the murder of Franz Ferdinand.

An Insubstantial
Pageant of Power

During the last half century, ruling a Balkan nation has not been a safe occupation. Before the end of World War II very few kings died a natural death while still in power. Courts ruled by bizarre and autocratic monarchs rose and fell with startling regularity, each time plunging their countries into fresh sufferings. Assassinations and abdications, treachery and reprisals brought an end to almost every reign. Even today, when the Communist control of the peninsula seems to ensure stability if not freedom, upsets are still possible. Under Tito, some critics of the regime have been killed or jailed. Albania has witnessed a succession of harsh purges. The cauldron is still bubbling.

MURDERED COUPLE, the Austrian Archduke Franz Ferdinand and his wife Sophie lie in state after their assassination in June 1914. Ironically, the Archduke was killed because the Serbs feared that his plans for giving South Slavs equal status in the Austro-Hungarian Empire challenged Serbian ambitions in the Balkan area.

CAPTURED ASSASSIN, Gavrilo Princip is led off *(left)* by Bosnian police after shooting Archduke Franz Ferdinand and his wife Sophie on June 28, 1914. The assassination, which precipitated World War I, took place in Sarajevo, the capital of Bosnia, an Austrian province at the time. Princip was an impassioned Serb nationalist.

FIERCE BRAWL ensues *(left)* as French soldiers close in on the assassin of King Alexander I of Yugoslavia beside the King's car in Marseilles on October 9, 1934. The assassin, Vlada Georgiev, was in the employ of Croatian and Macedonian separatists. Both groups were in violent opposition to Alexander's centralist régime.

SLAIN LEADER, Yugoslavia's Alexander I lies dead in his car in Marseilles *(below)*, surrounded by shocked witnesses. The terrorists who planned the murder were in league with Mussolini, who hoped to undermine Yugoslavia and encroach on its territory, and with the Hungarians, who wanted to regain holdings in Yugoslavia.

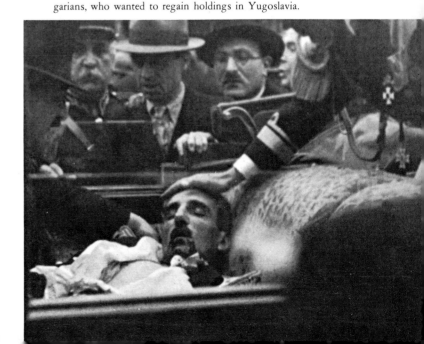

DASHING LOVER, King Carol II of Romania *(above, left)* appears at a rally in 1936 with his mother, Dowager Queen Marie, and son, Crown Prince Michael. Between 1927 and 1930, Carol had lived abroad with his mistress, Magda Lupescu, while Michael was King. In 1930 Carol ascended the throne, ruling until 1940, when Romanian leaders compelled him to abdicate again.

FAMILY GATHERING in Albania *(opposite)* comprises King Zog, his nephew Tati *(left)* and his three unmarried sisters, who were colonels in the Army. Originally the chieftain of an Albanian tribe, Zog first became Premier of the country, then King in 1928. His regime ended when Mussolini invaded Albania in 1939 and made Italy's Victor Emmanuel III King of Albania.

IRON DICTATOR Czar Boris III of Bulgaria receives a blessing from the Orthodox Archbishop of Sofia in 1937. Although Boris ascended the throne in 1918, he did not inaugurate his personal dictatorship until 1935. His shrewd, cynical reign ended in 1943, when he died under mysterious circumstances after visiting Hitler in Berlin and refusing to declare war on Russia.

UNPOPULAR REGENT, Prince Paul (*right*) confers with King Peter II of Yugoslavia. When Peter's father, Alexander I, was assassinated in 1934, Peter was only 11. His cousin Paul became Regent. Paul's alliance with Hitler in March 1941 so angered the Yugoslavs that they ousted him. Peter and his Government were forced to flee after Germany's attack the next month.

ERSTWHILE FRIENDS, Marshal Tito and his official biographer, Vladimir Dedijer *(right)*, appear together in 1953 at a ceremony in Slovenia. Shortly thereafter, Dedijer, who was a

ACCUSED PRELATE, Alojzije Stepinac *(left)* stands in a doorway near Zagreb after his release from prison in 1951. In 1946, Tito jailed Stepinac, then an archbishop, as a "Fascist collaborator." Although the Vatican appointed him a cardinal in 1952, Stepinac was still under surveillance when he died in 1960.

ROYALIST GENERAL, Draža Mihailović listens to charges of treason during his trial in 1946 before a military court in Belgrade. The prosecution charged that Mihailović, a violent anti-Communist who had led a pro-monarchy resistance group, had collaborated with Fascists. He was convicted and shot.

Partisan hero during World War II and later editor of the Communist Party's official newspaper, fell out of favor when he defended Milovan Djilas' right to criticize the Party bureaucracy.

INTRANSIGENT CRITIC, Milovan Djilas, with his sister *(left)* and his wife, leaves his trial in 1955. Once Tito's Vice President, Djilas fell from grace for writing articles critical of the Party. Since then he has been sent to prison three times for similar transgressions, serving a total of nine years in all.

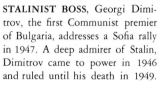

STALINIST BOSS, Georgi Dimitrov, the first Communist premier of Bulgaria, addresses a Sofia rally in 1947. A deep admirer of Stalin, Dimitrov came to power in 1946 and ruled until his death in 1949.

A GIFT OF BREAD causes Romania's Gheorghe Gheorghiu-Dej (*right*) to smile. Party leader for 20 years, he spent the decade prior to his death in 1965 leading Romania away from Soviet domination.

RUSSIA-ORIENTED Todor Zhivkov *(opposite)*, Premier of Bulgaria since 1962, visits with school children. Loyal to Soviet leaders, he has purged a number of Stalinists from Party and Government posts.

RARE APPEARANCE of Enver Hoxha *(right)*, dictator of Albania, draws crowds in Vlorë. Ordinarily, he and other Government leaders refuse to emerge from their closely guarded compound in Tirana.

Citizens of Belgrade admire a new fountain in Marx and Engels Square in the capital of Yugoslavia. The lighted building (background)

is the Federal Assembly, where the national parliament convenes.

5

Challenge to the Kremlin

IT is recorded in Sir Winston Churchill's war memoirs that one evening in Moscow, in the autumn of 1944, the British Prime Minister casually took up pencil and paper and attempted, in the company of Josef Stalin, to decide the fate of the Balkans.

"The moment was apt for business," Churchill writes, "so I said [to Stalin], 'Let us settle about our affairs in the Balkans. Your armies are in Rumania and Bulgaria. We have interests, missions, and agents there. Don't let us get at cross-purposes in small ways. So far as Britain and Russia are concerned, how would it do for you to have ninety per cent predominance in Rumania, for us to have ninety per cent of the say in Greece, and go fifty-fifty about Yugoslavia?'"

While his words were being translated, the Prime Minister put his suggested arrangements on a sheet of paper, neatly listing 90 per cent for Russia in Romania and 10 per cent for "the others." He allotted 75 per cent to the Soviet

Union in Bulgaria and 25 per cent to "the others."

The listing completed, Churchill pushed the paper across to Stalin, who had by then heard the translation. "There was a slight pause. Then [Stalin] took his blue pencil and made a large tick upon it, and passed it back to us. It was all settled in no more time than it takes to set down."

"It was all settled . . ." But of course, nothing was settled. Churchill implies that he almost instantly regretted drawing up the list. "Might it not," he recalls asking Stalin, "be thought rather cynical if it seemed we had disposed of these issues, so fateful to millions of people, in such an offhand manner? Let us burn the paper." There is no evidence that Stalin was in the slightest degree disturbed. Even then, in the brief conversational pause which Churchill records, Stalin must have been calculating how the agreement could be turned to advantage—or evaded.

AT first sight, there may seem little point in this sordid story. The bargain which Churchill struck in Moscow would prove illusory; the peoples of the Balkans—the most passionate and least malleable of human beings—had not been consulted at all. Moreover, no compromise with the Soviets was possible. The issue of postwar leadership in the Balkans was, in any case, very largely settled by October 1944. The Soviet armies had advanced deep into the heart of Eastern Europe, and with them, a new order had marched as well. Soviet political agents—backed by ample terror—were establishing the basis of Communist control.

Yet the story of this exercise in diplomatic futility foreshadows the history of the postwar Balkans—and it may be, more largely, of the postwar world as well. After 1946 the great power blocs would coalesce and the Cold War would begin. But the postwar years would be a period of passionate and fragmented nationalisms as well. These years would be an age of anti-empire in which, in a sense, the whole world would become Balkanized—violent, turbulent and unruly, as small states defied great

ones. Whatever the statesmen might believe, the true age of great-power settlements was dead. Even the United States and the Soviet Union would, in the years that lay ahead, find themselves curiously balked. They would be often incapable, for all their strength, of affecting the day-to-day course of political events.

THUS the essential political lessons of the postwar world would find an early expression in the Balkan arena: There, as the lines between East and West were firmly drawn at last, the shape of the Cold War would emerge. Britain, failing to impress its influence on the postwar Balkans, and finding the attempt to support the Greek Government against Communist-led guerrillas too much, would come to terms with its shrunken role in the postwar world and call in the United States. And Stalin's Russia, failing to understand the meaning of its own political slogans—slogans of people's wars, people's rights, people's aspirations—would find its dream of a universal Marxist empire broken on the intransigent nationalism of one small Balkan state.

In the beginning, of course, it seemed that the wily Stalin had won the game. The Soviets held all the trump cards. In 1944-1945 their armies overran the strategic heartland of central Europe and the Balkans, and their agents, the Communist parties, were all loyal to Moscow—the new Rome of proletarian revolution.

The story of the Communist seizure of power in the four Balkan states is a melancholy one. In Albania, where political life before the war had never advanced significantly beyond the tribal level and no true liberal politics existed, there was scarcely a transition period between the collapse of the German occupation and the imposition of a new Communist totalitarianism. Under the leadership of the former schoolteacher Enver Hoxha, the Albanian Communist Party—itself a satellite of the Yugoslav Communists, who seem to have been contemplating the annexation of the country—established a bloody authority. Hoxha, although hindered by intraparty jealousies and factionalism, ruthlessly extirpated the political opposition, such as it was, and by 1947 he had driven the military representatives of the United States and Britain from the country.

In Yugoslavia, controlled at the war's end by the powerful guerrilla army of Josip Broz Tito, there was scarcely more of a transition. A cynical wartime understanding with the exiled Royal Yugoslav Government became a dead letter only five months after the Soviet and Yugoslav armies entered Belgrade, when it became apparent that Tito was not going to permit the royalists any real voice in the country's affairs. More threatening to the postwar peace was the fact that Yugoslavia's grandiose imperial aspirations (in Albania, in the Italo-Yugoslav frontier zone of Trieste, and in the Austrian frontier province of Carinthia) came into conflict with the interests of the Western powers. Yugoslav armies threatened the British and American occupation forces in the Free Territory of Trieste; Yugoslavia was the chief base of support for the Greek Communist guerrillas threatening to sever the Mediterranean life line vital to Britain and the United States. In 1946 two unarmed American transport planes were brought down by the Yugoslav Air Force in what was clearly a calculated gesture of defiance.

IN the defeated Axis satellites of Bulgaria and Romania, the Communists were forced to proceed a little more cautiously than in Albania and Yugoslavia—for the United States and Britain were using the power of diplomatic recognition to attempt to bring about the establishment of freely elected governments. But by 1946-1947 the Communist parties, enjoying the protection of the Soviet armies, had been able to resort to the Communist political maneuver known as "salami tactics" —the day-to-day slicing off of the political opposition. The technique was to form coalition governments—"National" or "People's" Fronts—in which all "progressive" parties opposed the parties of "reaction." In these coalition governments, the ministerial posts were shared by the Communists and the non-Communists, who were already intimidated by scarcely veiled Soviet threats, in a fluid proportion which became steadily more favorable to the Communists and their agents. Typically, the Communists demanded the ministries of justice (the courts) and interior (the police). Eventually, these interim governments were succeeded by "elected" governments when the process of nationwide political intimidation had proceeded so far that rigged elections could be counted on to sweep a successor government, one even more heavily dominated by Communists, into office.

WHAT then invariably followed was a campaign of naked political threat against non-Communists serving in the coalitions, until one by one the fellow-traveling parties were absorbed by the Communists or driven into opposition. Eventually they were unmasked as "enemies of the people" and branded Fascist or reactionary. By 1947-1948, Communist control in the Balkans (and in all East-Central Europe) had become virtually complete.

This political conquest was a triumph of calculating and cruel politics, and it took its toll of brave men. There were moments of real drama. In Bulgaria in the spring of 1947, Nikola Petkov, leader of the non-Communist Agrarian Union party, was summarily arrested on the floor of Parliament after a long struggle against the encroaching power of the Communists and was taken away amid the screams of his friends and enemies. Petkov was hanged that autumn after a trumped-up treason trial, and with him, the hope of opposition in Bulgaria died too. More dramatic still was the trial in Yugoslavia of Tito's old enemy, Draža Mihailović. Mihailović comported himself in the dock with a sober dignity. His closing address to the court struck a note of genuine tragedy.

"I found myself in a whirl of events and strivings," he said. "I was confronted with the aims and tendencies of my own government. I was surrounded with all possible intelligence services . . . Destiny was merciless towards me when it threw me into the most difficult whirlwinds. I wanted much, I began much. But the whirlwind, the world whirlwind, carried me and my work away."

Mihailović was executed on July 17, 1946, and was buried in a criminal's grave.

It seemed, therefore, that within a few short years of the war's end Stalin had fulfilled all the imperial ambitions of the czars. From the Baltic in the north to the Adriatic in the south, the Soviet empire was docile and secure. The Soviet word was law in Bucharest, Sofia, Belgrade and Tirana—the ancient Balkan capitals which had been for centuries the longed-for booty of the Balkan diplomatic game.

No one believed, least of all the Soviet Union's opponents in the West, that a native force could arise to withstand the centralizing forces of the Soviet bloc. Everywhere the political opposition to the Soviets had been silenced. The organizations that had succeeded to power were self-consciously Marxist parties, denouncing nationalism as archaic and proclaiming a new proletarian internationalism.

CERTAINLY in the first postwar years everything seemed to favor the Soviet cause. The Balkan states coordinated their policies through Moscow and the newly established Communist Information Bureau, or Cominform, and began a process of slavish emulation of everything Soviet. Industry and trade were rapidly nationalized. "Kulaks"—the Russian term for rich peasants—were exorbitantly taxed. The much-heralded land-reform programs—and with them the whole concept of private farming—were compromised. The collective-farm system was founded; into the expanding collectives the poor and the "middle peasants" were enticed—and often coerced.

In the cities, ill-fed adolescents and the aged labored in "volunteer" work brigades. In the factories, workers who had credulously accepted the new movement and believed themselves members of a postwar proletarian elite found themselves exploited more mercilessly than ever. ("What is the difference between

capitalism and Communism?," a joke of the time asked. "Capitalism is the exploitation of man by man. In Communism it is the reverse.") Work norms climbed; living standards, always low in this backward region, plummeted. In the mountain villages, there were not even simple necessities like kerosene or matches. Eventually matters grew so desperate that angry peasants slaughtered their livestock in protest—and found themselves hauled away by the truckload to labor camps. The cities starved.

WITH only minor exceptions (and these were usually tactical concessions designed to allay the fears of opposition groups until they could be destroyed) the Balkan satellites thus re-created the essential political, economic and social institutions of Soviet life. In Yugoslavia, where the party leaders were especially arrogant, inflamed as they were by the success of their wartime resistance movement, the zeal to press forward rapidly with the social transformation of society reached notoriously brutal proportions. Unknown thousands were arrested for political crimes in Yugoslavia in 1947-1948.

Yet within this very zeal to emulate the Soviets lurked one clue to the future course of Balkan politics. Tito sought to accomplish in five years what his mentor Stalin had done in 10. A satellite politician, he saw in Albania a satellite of his own, and he pushed an aggressive, independent diplomacy against Greece, Austria and Trieste, as we have noted. Without consulting Stalin, he flouted the Americans. Moreover, his offenses were not merely assertions of national power against Western interests. The undisciplined and frequently brutal behavior of Soviet troops in Yugoslavia was criticized. As a Soviet note complained in March 1948: "Some said that the rules of the Soviet army were hidebound, stereotyped, and without value to the Yugoslav army." The note charged that Milovan Djilas, then head of the Agitation and Propaganda section of the Yugoslav Communist Party and later Vice President of the Federal Assembly, had insulted the Soviet Army at a session of the Yugoslav

Communist Party, alleging that Soviet officers were "from a moral standpoint, inferior to the officers of the British army."

Such insolence was galling enough to the Soviets; worse still, Tito negotiated, without consulting the Russians, for an alliance between Yugoslavia and Bulgaria.

When Stalin and Molotov became aware of the negotiations, they summoned representatives of the offending governments to Moscow and angrily demanded an explanation. The Bulgarian Premier, Georgi Dimitrov, abased himself, but the Yugoslavs said little. Djilas later wrote: "The substance of the meeting came drastically into view . . . no relations among the 'people's democracies' were permissible beyond the interests and without the approval of the Soviet Government. It became evident that to the Soviet leaders, with their great-power mentality (which found expression in the concept of the Soviet Union as 'the leading force of socialism') and especially with their cognizance that the Red Army had liberated Rumania and Bulgaria . . . Yugoslavia's lack of discipline and willfulness were not only heresy but the denial of the Soviet Union's 'sacred' rights."

IT was a clash of wills. Stalin, watching balefully from the Kremlin, noted the growing signs of ambition and unreliability among the Yugoslav leaders. His characteristic countermove was to attempt to subvert the Yugoslav Party, to turn its cadres against Tito and his clique of friends—Djilas, Edvard Kardelj, the foreign affairs expert, and Aleksandar Ranković, the boss of the Yugoslav secret police. The Soviet intelligence apparatus stepped up its efforts to recruit spies within the Yugoslav Army, the Yugoslav police, and the Party.

But Stalin had underestimated his enemy. The Soviets made few converts. What was more to the point, the Yugoslavs had learned the game of political conspiracy in a hard Balkan school. The Yugoslav police had been shadowing the Soviet "representatives" for months.

All through the opening months of 1948, relations between the two Communist parties deteriorated. The Western world, listening to the oft-repeated slogans of Socialist ideological unity, suspected nothing. Outwardly all was disciplined cooperation. The Yugoslav leaders continued to extol the Soviets in public; by and large, the controlled press of the Soviet bloc reciprocated the courtesies. But behind the scenes, the reality was something else.

THE conflict between the Yugoslavs and the Soviets—historically the first fissure in the fabric of Communist unity, foreshadowing the momentous Sino-Soviet conflict a decade later—seems in retrospect as inevitable as fate. The parties advanced inexorably into combat. Yet the true meaning of the quarrel—the blasting of the hope that a Communist international society could transcend conflict—eluded both sides. The Yugoslavs especially, although they refused throughout the months of deepening crisis to recant, seem to have been blind to the ultimate meaning of their heresy. When the Soviets denounced the Yugoslavs at one point during the crisis, it was, said Tito some years later to his official biographer, "as if a thunderbolt had struck me."

Neither party would or could concede. Stalin, spoiled by years of sycophancy, no doubt expected to the end that Tito would weaken. Eventually—sometime in the spring of 1948 —the antagonists passed the point of no return. On June 28, 1948, the anniversary both of the battle of Kosovo and of the assassination of Franz Ferdinand at Sarajevo, the Cominform issued its formal anathema against the heretics: "Considerably overestimating the internal, national forces within Yugoslavia . . . the Yugoslav leaders think that they can maintain Yugoslavia's independence and build Socialism without the . . . Soviet Union."

In this belief, the statement went on, the Yugoslav leaders were hopelessly wrong; Tito and his minions were called on to repent. "Should the present leaders of the Yugoslav Communist Party prove incapable of doing this, [the 'healthy elements' of the nation should] replace them. . . ." It was, of course, a barely disguised call for revolution. None came.

There is a danger of sentimentalizing the Yugoslav position in 1948. The image of David and Goliath leaps too readily to mind. For the sake of historic truth, it is important to understand that the Tito-Stalin conflict, in its origins, was a clash not of Stalinist imperialism with a national Communism, the latter of necessity a better and more humane ideology; it was the clash of *two* national Communisms, Yugoslav and Soviet, the one with the other.

Stalin had made Communism, a movement which had been at its inception a universal ideology, into a scarcely concealed instrument of Russian national interests. But Yugoslav Communism enjoyed no moral superiority over the Soviet brand. It was as narrow-minded, hardhearted, doctrinaire and imperialist (within its limited possibilities) as the Soviets' own. The practical distinction for the West lay in the nature of the combatants. The Soviet Union was a giant empire, a continental super-power. Yugoslavia was a small Balkan state with less than 16 million people—bellicose, threatening to its smaller neighbors, driven by a self-confident Communist Party—but the effect of Yugoslavia's schism was to weaken the larger Soviet bloc. For the West, fearful of the seemingly disciplined worldwide Communist movement arrayed against it, the Tito-Stalin break was a godsend; it was the first intimation of the erosion of Communist unity.

FOR the Titoists, the period after the break was a chancy one. The Yugoslavs had no friends—neither East nor West. But in time, the logic of the situation asserted itself. While Yugoslavia, in the years of its orthodox Communist precocity, had alienated the U.S. and Britain—the very countries that it now needed—it was luckier in its Western enemies than in its unforgiving Eastern ones. Between 1948 and 1950, there ensued a period of gingerly diplomatic maneuvering in which Yugoslavia and the Western powers explored each other's intentions. As much in fear of a kind of spiritual rape by the West as of the return of the old

economic colonialism which the Yugoslav Party's ideology warned against, the Titoists only slowly expanded trade contacts with the West. But they had no alternative: the Soviets had abruptly canceled virtually all trade and credits. How damaging this Soviet economic offensive was, the bare figures reveal. Yugoslav commerce with the Soviet bloc before the break amounted to almost half of the country's total foreign trade. By 1949 it had fallen to 13.7 per cent. The Yugoslav economy, already damaged by the war and the ineptitude of doctrinaire planners, was brought close to ruin.

Fortunately for the Yugoslavs, the West chose to intervene. Between 1949 and 1955 the U.S. made available credits of more than one billion dollars—$589 million in military aid (there were almost daily demonstrations in force by Yugoslavia's neighbors along the Hungarian, Romanian and Bulgarian frontiers) and $574 million in economic assistance.

ASSOCIATION with the West inevitably brought influences of a broader kind. Yugoslavia might assert its doctrinal independence of the West, it might insist that American, British and French economic and military aid be given wholly without conditions, but for all the fanaticism of the Yugoslav leadership, the rank-and-file of the Party and the youth came to yearn for a life of a different sort than that provided by a garrison state.

Yugoslavia, however unwillingly, was thrown into reliance on the West and, fighting for its life against the East, was forced to define itself in opposition to Stalinist orthodoxy. The result was that Yugoslavia's Communist leadership, observing the West at first hand, began to innovate—and the innovations proceeded almost uniformly in the direction of a greater humanity. By 1953, when Stalin died, Yugoslav Communism had come a considerable distance from its Stalinist origins. The nation was never so loyal and united as in its opposition to the Soviets. To mighty Soviet Russia a small Balkan nation had administered a stinging rebuke and a galling defeat.

An audience including a number of children attends a performance of "The Barber of Seville" at the Opera House in Iaşi, Romania.

With New Prosperity, a Fuller and Richer Life

Large cities in the Balkans have been vigorous cultural and academic centers for centuries. The universities and the institutions dedicated to music, theater and dance have had to weather so many storms that they have become tough. With the end of World War II, old Balkan cultural traditions revived, and the people are once again enjoying artistic and educational opportunities. The opera house in Bucharest, bombed in World War II, is thriving today.

In Belgrade, where formerly there were only two theaters, four new houses have opened since 1945. Today the sidewalk cafés are buzzing with conversation, and while there is no overabundance, life is easier. Prosperity has brought new interest in sports and other leisure-time pursuits. On dance floor and ski slope, and in the sunshine of beach resorts—away from the harsh *Realpolitik* of Marxism—people are finding a full measure of nonpolitical diversion.

A NEW LOOK *of elegance reflects Western influence and economic well-being*

TEENAGERS at a party in Sofia, Bulgaria, swing to the big beat of discothèque-style music, looking for all the world like their counterparts in London or New York. For the young, no curtain separates East and West.

THEATER-GOERS congregate at intermission on the lobby balcony of the handsome Palace Hall in Bucharest, Romania. The clean lines of the hall are in bright contrast to Communism's heavy Stalin-era architecture.

A GIRL SKIER, well turned out in sunglasses and ribbed, turtleneck sweater, prepares for a run down the slope at a ski lodge high in Bulgaria's Rhodope Mountains. Smart resorts such as this boom with winter vacationers.

YOUNG PEOPLE in ever-growing numbers avidly pursue studies and athletics

SURGERY LECTURE in Cluj, Romania, is attended by third-year students. Most Romanian universities give preference to applicants who have working-class or peasant backgrounds.

BIOCHEMISTRY STUDENTS examine test tubes *(left)* at the medical college in Tîrgu-Mureş, Romania. Established in 1946, the college already has more than 1,000 students.

AMATEUR GYMNASTS perform a balancing act during a sporting event in Bucharest. Romania's Communist Party operates physical fitness programs in every educational institution.

LAVISH RESORTS built in the last 10 years swarm with tourists from all over Europe

SITTING IN A BOOTH, guests drink beer at a bar in "Sunny Beach," a resort on Bulgaria's coast. A two-week vacation is inexpensive; Britishers, for example, pay less than $300, including transportation from London.

DANCING UNDER THE STARS, tourists crowd the patio of the Trimontium Hotel in Plovdiv, Bulgaria (*left*). The hotel, operated by the Government tourist bureau, caters to Bulgarians and foreigners alike.

LUNCHING IN THE CASINO, vacationers eat in an informal atmosphere at Sunny Beach (*opposite*). In the summer of 1963, when Sunny Beach first opened for business, the resort's 40 hotels were filled to capacity.

OUTDOOR THEATER is an attraction at Mamaia Beach, Romania's best-known Black Sea resort. The theater's acoustics are improved by tall slabs which shield the auditorium from a nearby hotel.

SUN WORSHIPERS congregate on the beach at Eforie in Romania *(below)*. Like the Bulgarian resorts on the Black Sea, Romanian vacation areas are all the result of a building boom in the last 10 years.

GLEAMING HOTELS surrounded by landscaped grounds and new roads line the shore of Mamaia Beach. The hotels face the salty Black Sea on one side and fresh-water Lake Siutghiol on the other.

GROUP SHOWERS of mineral water are used by bathers at Golden Sands Beach in Bulgaria. The resort not only caters to the foreign tourist trade but also provides rest homes for Bulgarian workers.

6

A Society Almost Free

FOR tourists in search of cloak-and-dagger adventure, there is no more disappointing experience than today's Italian-Yugoslav frontier at Trieste. What was once a major world tension point—like Berlin, a frontier between two armed camps, one slave and the other free, and a place fraught with peril to international peace—is now characterized by the routine formality of a perfunctory customs check. Not even a visa is required.

In place of the menacing post-World War II vista of watchtowers, tank traps, burned fields cleared for machine-gun fire, and barbed-wire fences, there is something incongruous and new—a traffic jam of motorscooters, Volkswagens, Fiat 600s, and even opulent Mercedes-Benzes waiting to cross the frontier. But only tourists in search of an Ian Fleming romance would complain; the Yugoslavs—and the Triestinos—who cross happily back and forth to visit do not. What has happened is simply this: the Iron Curtain has been transported some 350 miles to the east. The Iron Curtain once reached as far west as the Adriatic; in the Balkans today it follows the line of the Romanian-Bulgarian frontier.

Tito's Yugoslavia is a shock—a pleasant shock in a world accustomed to bad news. The reasons are manifold. Despite a somewhat un-even economic performance, Yugoslavia is his-tory's leading example of a semi-affluent Com-munist society; and it is also the first self-pro-claimed socialist state to adopt policies designed to promote individual satisfaction rather than purely collective well-being. Moreover, millions of foreigners have visited Yugoslavia in the past decade, bringing the freshness of outside ideas to the one-time garrison state. In 1967, the authorities even went so far as to abolish tourist visas; and Yugoslavs themselves can apply for—and receive—passports for foreign travel at any one of the many tourist agencies in the larger cities and towns.

TENS of thousands of Yugoslav citizens vis-it abroad—either for pleasure or to work for better wages in Italy, Austria or West Ger-many. The intellectual young of the country study abroad, and even when they do not, they are fully conversant with the work of avant-garde Western writers, artists and film directors. Popular recordings, from the Beatles to what-ever new outrage is current in the West, are also available; the Yugoslavs themselves play assiduous jazz. In the remote mountain villages of Bosnia and Montenegro, peasant children perform the obsessive ritual of the hula-hoop only a few years out of date. The country man-ufactures Italian Fiat cars and sells them—on the installment plan—to tired Party bureau-crats whose goading wives talk now of their "little dressmakers," buy cake mixes in super-markets and gossip when they meet at the thea-ter. (Milovan Djilas, perennial Party rebel, originally fell from grace as the result of his sharp attack on Yugoslavia's new class snob-bery in a magazine article entitled "Anatomy of a Moral," in which figured, only thinly dis-guised, the wives of high-ranking Party offi-cials. He was ousted from the Party's Central Committee in 1954, subsequently to be repeat-edly jailed and released.)

Dispirited Communist husbands have be-gun to retaliate in kind—shedding their super-annuated *partizankas*, as the dedicated women who fought alongside them in the Partisan days are known, in favor of younger, prettier, less ideologically marked wives—as often as not the daughters of the "reactionary" urban classes they had expected to wipe out in 1945-1946. There is a social reconciliation at work within today's Yugoslavia; the two old social enemies, Communists and bourgeoisie, are growing to-gether. Time has begun to heal the wounds.

YUGOSLAV industry grew for a time at a rapid clip; between 1952 and 1962 indus-trial production doubled. But the record of re-cent years has been less impressive. The untried combination of socialist institutions and fea-tures of a free market economy caused un-familiar problems. During the mid-1960s, for instance, the country experienced severe infla-tion and a general economic downturn, result-ing in new and drastic reforms.

Under the Yugoslav system, now widely imi-tated in the Soviet orbit, the Government has converted nationalized industry from centrally run state-enterprises to separate, competing units expected to show profits. They are in-dividually managed by workers' councils, free to make their own decisions.

It is possible today to buy a good meal at a good restaurant in Yugoslavia, or to buy a good suit or dress or camera or television set at prices not hopelessly beyond the reach of the common man. But viewed dispassionately, the process of modernization and liberalization at work in Yugoslavia is not uniformly pretty. An expense-account aristocracy has prolifer-ated; the nightclubs of Belgrade and Zagreb are not easily distinguishable from comparable expense-account establishments in Chicago or Munich. The social landscape, Marxism to the contrary, is essentially the same; the overfed businessmen are there, the overdressed wives— and sometimes the underdressed call girls. The Government—not very seriously—likes to deny that beggars and prostitutes exist, but blatant evidence suggests the contrary. The call girls are merely cleared out of the capital on the occasion of any particularly important state function. During the international conference in Belgrade in the autumn of 1961 which such luminaries as Nehru, Nasser, Sukarno and Nkrumah attended, the girls were rounded up by the police and packed off to farms south of Belgrade. They returned two weeks later sporting tans. There is no reason, of course, why Yugoslavs should be called upon to practice a sterner morality than others keep. But Yugoslavia's social vices are seldom worn with grace. The tradition of the peasant morality is still too strong among these people; when they sin, they do it badly. The *dolce vita* may, in the last analysis, be a bleak one; but Yugoslavia's version —the *sladak život*—is often clumsy to boot.

Engrossed as they are in the miracle of near affluence, Yugoslavs are, however, no more inclined than Americans or Western Europeans to vex themselves overmuch with ultimate questions. On any fine evening in spring, strolling crowds fill the streets of Belgrade, Zagreb or Sarajevo; there are pretty girls in beehive hairdos and too much mascara; gangling peasant boys in field-gray army uniforms and partisan caps, shyly eying the girls; middle-aged couples solemnly taking the air. From 10 in the morning on any fine day the cafés are jammed by an ever-shifting, wildly gesticulating mob of Party bureaucrats in town from the provinces; "state" businessmen haggling over deals; unpublished authors and unemployed journalists; avant-garde painters; clerks who have made a momentary and perilous escape from countinghouses and stock rooms; actresses "between" films; the omnipresent girls. Viewing such a scene, the observer

realizes with a start that Yugoslavia is a Mediterranean country; it belongs to the region of the sun. Its merriment has been blotted out too often in the tragic past.

But the memories of anxiety and deprivation are still fresh, and for a good many years after the break with the Soviets in 1948, the Yugoslav experiment in a more humanistic and bearable Communism seemed a chancy thing. If it has succeeded—if Yugoslavia today is a phenomenon in the Communist world that supplies guarded evidence for the hope that even the worst tyrannies may, with a little luck, grow less harsh in time—the achievement is largely one man's. That man is Josip Broz Tito, a curiously contradictory figure—both ruthless and benign, cruel and amiable, doctrinaire and pragmatic.

His early origins were for years obscure; indeed during World War II he was widely believed by his enemies to be a Communist fiction, a Croatian (or Serbian) plot, even a woman. But it is now known that he was born in 1892 of mixed Croatian and Slovenian parentage and that he worked as a machinist before World War I. He was drafted into the Austro-Hungarian Army just before the war, was subsequently taken prisoner on the Russian front, and thereafter played a small part in the Bolshevik Revolution.

In 1935 he became a Comintern agent, traveling through Central Europe and the Balkans as an *illegalets*, or underground worker. (A plausible tale has it that he badly frightened the mother of a co-conspirator with whom he once hid out in Zagreb. "Listen, my son,"

HARSH ATTACKS ON PARTY CHIEFS

In *Anatomy of a Moral*, a 1954 attack on Yugoslavia's leaders, the Communist Party rebel Milovan Djilas tells the story of a girl who marries a wartime resistance leader. This and similar attacks brought about Djilas' imprisonment. Below is an excerpt.

No one bothered to ask himself, nor could they all in their exclusiveness ask, who the bride really was, where she'd come from, who her parents, brothers and sisters were. The only important factor for this set was that she belonged to a different social stratum, that she had "illegally" sneaked into the group of people who had fought in the war, won the power we now wield and the freedom we now enjoy, and who, now that the war is over, all occupy ranking positions in the state, have automobiles, travel by pullman, get their food and clothing at special stores, spend their holidays in secluded villas, summer resorts and spas, and who, on the basis of all this, have gradually convinced themselves that they are exceptionally meritorious and that all of this privilege is so very natural and logical that only fools and obdurate enemies could have any doubts about it.

the old lady said, "stay away from this one. His razor is German, his soap is Czech, his shirt is from Moscow. He's a bad one.") In 1937 he was appointed by Moscow to reorganize the demoralized and shattered Communist Party of Yugoslavia, whose leadership had been virtually wiped out in the Stalinist purges of the mid-1930s.

WE have seen how the clandestine network Tito organized so successfully became the foundation of his ruthless and triumphant wartime resistance movement, and how he came into conflict with Stalin. It is possible to discern in this drama the inevitable workings of historical fate; no doubt the Yugoslav Communists would prefer to believe that the Tito-Stalin conflict represents an example of the immutable laws of Marxist determinism. But Marx's economic determinism does not allow for the role of personality, and it gives short shrift to national—and personal—pride. It is clear that what occurred in 1948 when Tito and Stalin clashed was the result of the blending of two elements. The powerful personality of one man—Tito—interacted with the powerful personality of another—Stalin—and the two played out a drama that was bigger, far bigger, than either. Stalin expressed Russian nationalism at its most narrow-minded and ruthless; Tito expressed the nationalism of a small Balkan nation at its most unbending. Both men were fundamentally nationalists. But while Stalin's efforts so to consolidate his country as to make it a formidable imperial power stultified Russia's great artistic and intellectual heritage and caused a terrible deformation of Russian life, Tito's chauvinism had the reverse effect: it cut Yugoslavia off from the baleful effects of association with the East and threw it into renewed contact with the happier influences of the West.

But such improvements in the quality of Yugoslav life after the 1948 break came only slowly. The first reaction of the Yugoslav leaders after their expulsion from the Soviet camp was to prove themselves—to assert an even more rigid and doctrinaire Marxist orthodoxy. The tempo of collectivization increased after the break, police terror deepened, and living standards—already abysmal—fell still more. The Yugoslav leaders were determined to prove that Stalin's charges of heresy were false. But as the Soviets began to resort to military threats against the country's security, Yugoslavia had no choice but to reverse its foreign policies. Yugoslav trade, for example, was wholly redirected. In 1953, the year Stalin died and only five years after the break, Yugoslavia's major trading partners were West Germany, Italy and the United States. Britain and France added $80 million to the $377 million in economic aid granted by the United States.

The process of liberalization, of course, was not only slow but uncertain. Such innovations as decollectivization, the decentralization of economic planning, the demand that the new and semi-independent factories and trading enterprises function at an actual profit, the freeing of the majority of political prisoners and the marked improvement in living standards were of course popular. But apart from the natural desire to prove wrong the Soviet charges of being "soft on capitalism," such liberalizing changes were profoundly disturbing to the doctrinaire minds within the Communist Central Committee. At lower levels of the Yugoslav Party the process of democratization threatened the prerogatives of those Party hacks whose chief qualifications for their posts of privilege were a blind loyalty to an ill-understood Communism and a record of early adherence to the holy cause. But the process of liberalization, once begun, could not truly be halted. It had something of the inevitability of a natural phenomenon.

PUT another way, the old character of Yugoslavia reasserted itself. As the western Balkans had so many times in history figured as an uneasy transition zone—the frontier between Byzantium and the West, between the Eastern Orthodox Church and Roman Catholicism, between Slav and German—so once again Yugoslavia after 1948 expressed another conflict of traditions and influences. This time it was the clash between Communist orthodoxy and the liberal political, economic and social system of the modern West.

There is no denying the improvement, by Western standards, that has taken place economically and politically in Yugoslavia since 1948. However, fundamental discords remain, not the least of them the old, poisonous antagonism existing between the six separate national groups within the country. Another is the rift between the orthodox Communists and those who favor liberalization. Both these conflicts were visible during the top-echelon upheaval that took place in the summer of 1966, when the Vice President and heir-apparent to Tito, Aleksandar Ranković, a Serb, was forced to resign all his posts. He was accused of using the predominantly Serb-staffed secret police in an attempt to frustrate the implementation of economic reforms. The police had even gone so far as to install listening devices in Tito's private quarters. As a result of this scandal, police powers were curbed. Nevertheless, while private conversation in Yugoslavia is now relatively free, and writers and artists may practice any avant-garde style they choose, political action against the regime can lead to swift punishment—as the young rebel Mihajlo Mihajlov learned in 1966 when he sought to publish an opposition journal and was speedily jailed.

THERE are curious ways, too, in which Yugoslav political life, for all its undoubted superiority to the political life of the more orthodox Communist states, retains some features of the uglier past largely outgrown in the post-Stalin Soviet bloc. Foremost of these archaic features is the way the nation adheres to the old "cult of personality"—a term which in the Communist world signifies the quasi-deification of the political leader. Soviet leaders have long accepted a less grandiose role than Yugoslavia's Tito is accustomed to play. Tito is still very much the national hero, the charismatic leader sprung from the wartime resistance movement. "Tito, Tito, little white flower, beloved by all the youth," the starveling youth brigades used to sing. The starveling brigades are gone, but the song can still be heard today, for Tito is a genuinely popular leader in his country, despite his ideological limitations. There are features of Yugoslav life (modern art is one, student Existentialists are another) which cause him genuine pangs—and move him to sometimes unreasonable outbursts. But Tito is a success—widely respected abroad—and the nation, whatever its political opinions may be, respects him as the incarnation of its difference from the rest of the world.

IF traces of a more somber and less appealing past do not quite dissolve on closer acquaintance with the country, they do shrink to size. The sober truth about Yugoslav progress since 1948 is impressive: in the years since the nation's expulsion from the Cominform, Yugoslavia has evolved into what can be described with only slight exaggeration as an "almost free society." At least it is possible to hope realistically that the process of improvement will, despite temporary setbacks, go on.

Hardly less significant was the effect of the Tito-Cominform break on the Soviet bloc itself. Early Titoism, we have seen, had little positive content, but its single-minded insistence on national separateness was the element actually most dangerous to the Stalinist empire in Eastern Europe. After the break, the Soviets were driven to bloody extremes to establish their supremacy. In the satellites the sin of nationalism was to be destroyed root and branch, and after 1948, the Soviets embarked on a savage witch hunt against "nativists" like Wladyslaw Gomulka in Poland and László Rajk in Hungary. In Romania, Lucretiu Pătrăşcanu was the victim of a Soviet-sponsored purge early in 1948, even before the Tito-Cominform quarrel broke into the open. There were bloody anti-Titoist purges in Bulgaria and Albania as well.

Such savagery had the desired effect. For five years it seemed that the poison of nationalism had been countered. The leaders of Bulgaria and Albania joined happily in the campaign, and they brought to bear on it something more than Marxist indignation at Tito's nationalist heresy. Their anti-Titoist campaign exploited the powerful nationalism of the people of Bulgaria and Albania, who were fundamentally anti-Yugoslav as well as anti-Titoist. The Yugoslav attack on the Soviets was thus easily contained in the Balkans, although it was not so well contained in satellites like Poland, where no anti-Yugoslav sentiment existed for the Soviets to exploit.

With Stalin's death in 1953, all this changed. The new Soviet effort was aimed at abating diplomatic tensions—the Balkans had, in effect, teetered on the brink of war for some five years—and at courting power and influence in the neutralist states of Africa and Asia, where Tito had also been seeking friends. The conflict with Yugoslavia was consequently an embarrassing liability at a time when the Soviet leaders were proclaiming a new policy of peaceful coexistence. Even more, Stalin as the great *Vozhd,* or leader, might endure the humiliation of Tito's defiance, but Stalin's uneasy heirs could not. And to be sure, the new leaders hoped to draw Tito back into the fold.

THE result was a stunning decision by Nikita Khrushchev and Nikolai Bulganin, then governing the U.S.S.R. in uneasy alliance. They would end the quarrel—and they would end it, so it seemed, essentially on Tito's terms. Arriving at Belgrade airport on May 26, 1955, Khrushchev was his most effusive: "Dear Comrade Tito. . . . The peoples of our countries are linked by ties of long brotherly friendship and joint struggle. . . . We sincerely regret what has happened. . . . We have studied assiduously the materials on which the serious accusations and offenses directed at that time against the leaders of Yugoslavia were based. The facts show that these materials were fabricated by enemies of the people. . . ."

It was a self-abasing speech, and also cynical, shameless and astute. Nevertheless, while the performance was skillful, it was one for which the Soviets would later pay dearly. It was for Khrushchev a deep humiliation. Soviet prestige could not survive it uncompromised. One might even say that the revolutionary upheavals which shook Eastern Europe in the autumn of 1956 derive in part from this event.

THE record of Soviet-Yugoslav relations in recent years has been too complex to detail here. Sometimes they have been bad, sometimes good. But no matter how good their relations may appear on the surface, a state of tension remains. The Russians would like to reincorporate the Yugoslav heretics into their bloc, but that bloc in many ways (and partly as a result of Yugoslav unorthodoxy) no longer truly functions. The Yugoslav leaders' terms for full reconciliation, in any case, are too steep: they would mean the end of Russia's accustomed authority as first among equals.

The Yugoslav leaders of the conservative stamp—and Tito, who has largely exhausted his capacity for innovation, is perhaps the most prominent among them—are profoundly disturbed by the growth of what they consider antisocial trends within their country, specifically by the influx of Western skepticism and social standards and by the loss of the old stern morality that animated the Partisan movement in its years of battle. To counterbalance the West, such Yugoslav leaders yearn for closer association with the East. But again the price is too high; to enter the Eastern camp unequivocally would mean to cut Yugoslavia off from daily contact with the invigorating stimuli of the Western world on which so many of the healthy features of Yugoslav life depend.

As for Titoism itself, only the future will reveal its ultimate course. But for Yugoslavia to reverse itself and return to the austere life which prevailed before the Cominform break is a practical impossibility. The zealots to fight for this second revolution simply do not exist: there are only a few Party fanatics left in Yugoslavia today, and they are growing old. The young simply do not care.

The managing board of a workers' council controlling railways in Zagreb, Yugoslavia, meets to discuss wages and working conditions.

Daring Economic Policies in the Socialist Camp

Although the Balkan nations have embraced socialism, they have increasingly adopted economic policies independent of those of the Soviet Union. Russian theorists, for example, had urged that Romania and Bulgaria hold back on industrial development and supply raw materials and farm products to the industrialized nations of the Soviet bloc. However, Romania is rapidly industrializing, and while Bulgaria is still subservient to Russia, it has recently followed Romania in expressing a desire for increased trade with the West. Romania is not only disregarding Russia's economic dictates but is also friendly with China and Albania. Yugoslav plants, even though nationalized, operate under the management of the workers, sell on a competitive market—and perform more efficiently than Russian factories.

MASS OUTPUT, which lowers costs, enables new factories to compete on Western European markets

AUTOMATED OPERATION in a textile factory *(left)* in Leskovac, Yugoslavia, requires only one girl to put nylon thread onto spools after dyeing. The new plant, with its nonobjective murals *(background)*, is operated by 40 workers in four shifts.

QUALITY TESTS at a tractor factory in Braşov, in Romania *(opposite)*, determine how well engines will perform after they leave the plant. The factory produces all of the nation's tractors and exports to more than 20 countries, many in the West.

CONSTRUCTING A PATTERN, workers in a machine-tool factory near Belgrade, Yugoslavia, make a mold for casting metal. Wages are from $40 to $67 monthly, high for the Balkans.

WELDING A SEAM, laborers in Bucharest, Romania, fit together sections of a railroad tank car (*right*) in the metal works of one of the largest rolling-stock plants in the Balkans.

TIGHTENING A BOLT, two technicians adjust a wheel assembly at the tractor plant in Braşov, Romania, a country that has made dramatic advances in producing steel and machinery.

7

The Spreading Nationalist Fever

OF the four Balkan nations which are the subject of this book, two—Yugoslavia and Albania—are openly in schism from the Soviet Union, latest of the series of empires which have attempted to impose their sway over the Balkans' nonmalleable peoples. Yugoslavia and Albania defy the Kremlin and preach alternative orthodoxies. One Balkan country—Romania—is gradually severing its economic and political ties to the Communist bloc. Only Bulgaria seems for the moment in accord with Soviet policy, and even there the future is unclear. What the Russians are facing is a resurgence of nationalism in their satellites—a

development perhaps inevitable in an era of "peaceful coexistence" in which the Soviets feel compelled to keep disputes with formerly docile puppets confined to the arena of argument and economic pressure. Soviet reluctance to resort to military intervention is resulting in a withering of control over the empire.

The new image of "teacher and leader" projected by the Soviet Union in the postwar years was for the Balkans only old-fashioned Russian imperialism writ large. After Yugoslavia, the first of the Balkan countries to break away was Albania, that nation of intense feelings which Nikita Khrushchev is rumored to have contemptuously dismissed as "a place for goats." The conflict between Albania and Russia was, however, slow in developing. The first effect of the break between Yugoslavia and Moscow in 1948 was to strengthen Albania's loyalty to Moscow, since Yugoslavia was Albania's feared neighbor and Albania saw the conflict as an opportunity to break free of a "protector" whose concern for the country threatened to end in Albania's outright annexation. The scarcely concealed Yugoslav intention in the immediate postwar years had been to annex Albania as a federal republic, adding Albania's 1,175,000 citizens to the sizable Albanian minority then dwelling in Yugoslavia, largely in the "autonomous" region of Kosovo-Metohija. In Albania itself, meddlesome Yugoslav advisers acted with outspoken arrogance.

ALBANIA was thus in the humiliating position of being a subsatellite—a "satellite's satellite"—a fact which was not lost on the Russians. In *Conversations with Stalin,* Milovan Djilas told of the sarcastic questions put to the Yugoslavs by Soviet officials: "Why were the Yugoslavs forming joint-stock companies with the Albanians when they refused to form the same in their own country with the USSR? Why were they sending instructors to the Albanian Army when they had Soviet instructors in their own? How could Yugoslavs provide experts for the development of Albania when they themselves were seeking experts from abroad? How was it that all of a sudden Yugoslavia, itself poor and underdeveloped, intended to develop Albania?" Despite the sarcasm, the U.S.S.R. apparently had no serious objection to Yugoslavia's imperial designs. In January 1948, Stalin had told Djilas: "We have no special interest in Albania. We agree to Yugoslavia's swallowing Albania . . . the sooner the better!"

The Albanians had no desire to be swallowed. The Yugoslavs might talk sanctimoniously of their disinterested aid to their tiny neighbor, but the fact remained that the price of Yugoslav aid was ultimate annexation. A bloody purge of

pro-Yugoslav elements took place when Albania followed the Soviet lead in the break with Yugoslavia in 1948. And hostile as most Albanians no doubt were to the harsh regime of Premier Enver Hoxha, the plump, sybaritic Secretary-General of the Albanian Communist Party, the people and the Party leaders at least shared a common desire to be rid of foreign rule.

What the Yugoslavs had forgotten, in other words, was that Albania was a Balkan state too. It was poor and abysmally backward, but it was proud, even if the illiteracy rate in 1945 was estimated at 80 per cent and its death rate was among the highest in Europe—the Albanians themselves say, "God loves Albania because it has changed so little since the Creation." Under Italian tutelage before World War II, industry had scarcely developed at all.

After the break with Yugoslavia, Albania became Russia's most slavish satellite. Stalin himself became a kind of mythic hero symbol to the Albanians; towering statues of him rose all over the country. With them came Soviet technicians and development funds. A number of factories and a hydro-electric power plant were built with Soviet aid. Heavily dependent on the aid, the Albanians were highly grateful. They might be small, but the U.S.S.R. and its mighty leader protected them against the capitalist "wolves" (the United States, Britain and Greece) and the Titoist "jackals." Russian submarine bases were constructed on Albania's Adriatic coast.

A CONSEQUENCE of this situation was that the Soviet position in Albania was secure—as long as Yugoslavia remained a Soviet enemy. But when two years after Stalin's death Khrushchev visited Belgrade to repair relations with the Yugoslavs, his action automatically triggered a reaction of fear—and even of panic—in Tirana, the Albanian capital. Tito was known to be demanding the removal of those satellite leaders who had been most violent in their attacks on him in the aftermath of his break with Stalin. Hoxha had been among the most vehement of Tito's foes. To him and his ruthless colleague, Mehmet Shehu, who assumed the premiership in 1954, the fate that awaited them—arrest, disgrace, imprisonment and possible execution—seemed all too clear. By calming the Soviet-Yugoslav conflict, Khrushchev succeeded in launching a new Soviet-Albanian political war.

The quarrel became intensely bitter—the imperial interests of the Soviet Union had collided with the demonic pride of one small and despised Balkan people. The Albanian leaders spoke out of a deep-rooted anxiety. The Soviet leaders, on the other hand, could not brook a basic political challenge from a minuscule nation only one fourth the size of America's bête noire, Cuba. And as has so often been the case in Balkan history, a small cause easily became a far larger one, for Albania did not have to remain isolated. It soon joined in an incongruous alliance with the giant of the Marxist lands—Communist China. In the late 19th Century, the improbable Montenegrins used to boast that "We and the Russians are 160 million strong." Today the Albanians boast that they and the Chinese are 700 million—and growing every day.

The full facts of the genesis of the Albanian-Soviet quarrel are not known. All that is clear is that in early 1956, Khrushchev, anxious to see his de-Stalinization policy adopted throughout Eastern Europe, found it in his own interests to meet Tito's price for friendship.

Two of Tito's vociferous enemies among the satellite leaders—Mátyás Rákosi, dictator of Hungary, and Vulko Chervenkov, dictator of Bulgaria—were ignominiously removed from office. Apparently only the Hungarian revolt

A RARE LOOK AT TIRANA

James Cameron, a British foreign correspondent, is one of the handful of Western newsmen who have been allowed to enter Albania since World War II. Below is an excerpt from his description of the capital of Tirana.

Down past New Albania Boulevard, down past Scanderbeg Square, where the vast statue of Stalin brooded over the . . . banners demanding long life for the worker's state, Tirana petered out gently into a tangle of wayward little streets and lanes of unmistakable poverty and increasing charm . . . there strolled the sort of Albanians one would not have thought ever to see outside a "fête folklorique." Half the people wore the drab serge of a normal urban proletariat, but the other half, without any kind of self-consciousness at all, swaggered around in . . . the enormous baggy pantaloons of the Muslim highlander. Albania must be one of the few countries left where what is known as peasant costume is in fact worn by peasants. It gave the back streets of Tirana a wonderfully rakish air.

in the autumn of 1956, and the brutal Soviet intervention which caused another cooling-off in Soviet-Yugoslav relations, saved Hoxha and Shehu. Even so, they were uneasy.

When Soviet-Yugoslav relations became warm again, Hoxha and Shehu again seemed in danger, only to be saved by still another breakdown in the off-again, on-again relationship between the two larger powers. By 1960, the Albanian leaders had become desperate enough to seek the protection of Communist China, which was then beginning its open attack on Soviet leadership under the guise of condemning Tito's "revisionism." Khrushchev was quick to undertake a counterattack against China and its new ally. In June he granted an interview to a Greek Leftist, and promised to take up with the Albanians the plight of the Greek minority in southern Albania. His words implied the possibility of a partition or rectification of frontiers— to Albania's disadvantage. Further to accentuate the element of threat, that summer the Soviets sharply cut back on economic aid—both to Peking and to Albania. In Tirana itself, the Russians tried, but failed, to carry out a coup d'état against Hoxha's regime.

From then on, Soviet-Albanian relations followed a steady downward path. In the fall of 1960, Hoxha and Shehu went to Moscow to attend an international conference of 81 Communist Parties, called to discuss the growing dispute between Russia and China. Placing Albania squarely behind China, Hoxha delivered a violent denunciation of the Soviet leadership.

Albania, Hoxha told the startled delegates, was only a small nation, but it would not, as

Khrushchev had demanded, "choose between 200 million Russians and 650 million Chinese." In a voice cracking with emotion, he complained bitterly about Soviet tactics. Albania had been wracked by earthquake, floods and drought, but the Soviets had cruelly withheld help. Famine had stalked Albania, but the U.S.S.R. had been evasive. It had promised, after nearly two months' delay, only 10,000 tons of wheat instead of the needed 50,000. "The Soviet rats," he concluded, "were able to eat while the Albanian people were dying of hunger; we were asked to produce gold."

REPORTEDLY Khrushchev purpled with fury. "You have emptied a bucket of dung on my head," he bellowed at Hoxha. Hoxha and Shehu, perhaps fearing the consequences of Hoxha's speech, left precipitately for Tirana. Shortly thereafter, the Albanians ostentatiously celebrated the birthday of Stalin, in direct challenge to Khrushchev, who had staked his reputation on making Stalin the scapegoat for the failures of Soviet policy.

Early the next year, the Albanians charge, the Soviets abruptly withdrew their oil technicians from Albania: the Soviets allege that the Albanians ordered the technicians to leave. In March 1961, the Soviet Union announced that it was canceling all economic aid, and by September, all Soviet and Eastern bloc technicians and aid personnel had left. Even the Soviet submarines were called home. By the early 1960s the breach was complete: the Soviets withdrew their entire diplomatic mission from Albanian soil. The Soviets' loyal allies, with the pointed exception of the Romanians, were threatening Tirana with severance of diplomatic relations. Within the Communist bloc, only the Chinese and their Asian satellites openly sided with the Albanians.

Looking back on it, the clash seems to have been irreconcilable, and made even more bitter by having been enlarged to worldwide dimensions. For Khrushchev to have apologized to the Albanians—and by implication to the Chinese—would have been a political misstep

that could only have speeded his fall. Once again, a Balkan controversy had cut loose from its moorings—its rational limits of time and place—to disturb the world.

In the northeast corner of the Balkans—in Romania—the challenge to the Kremlin's authority takes a different form. Albanian Communism is neo-Stalinist and austere; Romania, although still under control of the Party, has taken important steps toward internal relaxation. The Romanian challenge to Moscow expresses the Romanian past: it is intelligent, cynical and by no means quixotic. It is political (to a minor degree) and not military at all. Romania's heresy is of necessity discreet: while Albania may challenge Soviet power with greater confidence because of the country's geographical isolation, Romania, after all, shares a common border with the Soviets.

Thus the Romanian dissent has been more subtle than the Albanian, and largely confined to the realm of economic relations within the Soviet orbit. But this subtle challenge is all the more unanswerable by Moscow because neither a refusal to buy Soviet or East German machine tools, nor a self-assertive demand to press on with the industrialization of the country—thus upsetting Soviet plans for bloc-wide economic planning—is sufficient reason for the Soviets to send in their tanks in this loudly advertised period of peaceful coexistence.

WHAT has happened in Romania in recent years is of immense importance; it signals the development of a rabid economic nationalism, which is going counter to Soviet wishes. In its effort to industrialize, Romania has increasingly turned to the West for technical expertise and the most modern machinery, such as the nuclear research reactor it purchased from Great Britain in 1966. What has happened is well attested by the statistics: Romanian foreign trade with the Communist bloc declined steadily, from 79.3 per cent of its total exports in 1959 to little more than 50 per cent a few years later. These are the official Romanian figures. However, trade with the Soviet bloc is calculated in inflated prices. An adjustment of official figures to bring them into line with the real value of trade would reveal that in fact by the mid-1960s less than half of Romania's foreign commerce was being conducted with the East.

THUS barely 15 years after the establishment of Comecon, the Soviet-sponsored Council for Mutual Economic Assistance, Romania was probably trading more with West Germany, Italy, France, Britain and Austria than with its Communist "partners." It is the function of Comecon to coordinate the economic activities of the East European bloc. Originally, Soviet policy had encouraged each country to attempt to achieve economic self-sufficiency. In the late 1950s the theme became "socialist division of labor," with each of the countries specializing in sharply delineated areas of production under the general direction of Comecon. The supra-national control that would be necessary to realize such a plan, as well as the economic dislocations that it would bring about, have prompted murmurs of protest in the Soviet bloc countries, but only Romania has publicly refused to go along.

Romania's assigned role in the Comecon plan would have meant the abandonment of its industrialization plans and the perpetuation of its role as a supplier of petroleum, food and timber to the Soviet bloc. The Romanian Party leaders were determined to push ahead with industrialization. Their country was well endowed with the raw materials needed for an industrial economy, and they refused to bow to pressures from the already industrialized nations within the bloc to remain a "garden for the socialist states." Moreover, when the Romanians started to import the heavy machinery needed for their new factories, they soon found that Communist-bloc suppliers like East Germany and Czechoslovakia could not compete with Western suppliers in quality, price and terms. Consequently, they shifted their purchases to the West.

Charged with "economic egoism" at a Come-

con summit meeting in 1962 which considered complaints from Czechoslovakia and East Germany about the shift to the West in Romanian trade, the Romanians counterattacked by recalling how their country had been bled by the Soviets through the device of the Sovroms, "joint" Soviet-Romanian economic enterprises, which had been dissolved only after Stalin's death. They read a list of contracts never honored; they cited the fact that Romania in 1962 was required to pay 1957 prices for Polish coal, although the world market price had fallen by two thirds. They noted in addition that Romanian corn was sold to Poland at prices below world rates to fatten Polish pigs for sale to the West for hard currency which the Romanians could have used themselves. Instead of meekly apologizing, the Romanians only continued their resolve to follow an independent course.

The main goal of Romania's industrial drive has been to develop the metallurgical industries, and the keystone of expansion is a new steel complex at Galați on the Danube. Scheduled for completion in 1970, the Galați works are expected to produce four million tons of steel annually out of a scheduled national total of 7.5 million tons. Many of the Galați installations are being supplied by an Anglo-French consortium, and West German and Austrian firms share in the construction of the giant mill. The needed iron ore, the Romanians state blandly, will certainly be forthcoming from the brotherly Soviet Union. But as a precaution, the Romanians have talked with India and Brazil about possible imports.

THE Romanian optimism is staggering. By 1975 the Romanian engineers envision producing 10 times the 1959 output of electrical power. By that date they also expect to have extended the national power grid sufficiently to complete rural electrification. Romania claims to be the third largest exporter of oil-drilling equipment in the world; Romanian equipment is in the field as far away as India and Argentina.

The Romanian economy has grown at a startling pace since the launching of an ambitious

15-year-development program in 1960. During the first five years of the plan, the country's industrial growth rate averaged 15 per cent, the highest in Europe, while the growth rate of its manufacturing industry was the third highest in the world—after Taiwan and Japan, both beneficiaries of generous U.S. aid. Romania's performance far outdistanced that of any other country in the East bloc. Clearly, Romania is in the midst of a boom. The tempo of the industrial effort is almost palpable—and, despite the fact that the heavy investments in industrialization have kept living standards low, so is the great pride which Romanians of all classes show in their country's dynamism and growth.

In an effort to improve their bargaining position against Soviet pressures for economic conformity, the Romanians have recently been paying increasing attention to the rift between Russia and China. By giving some support to the Chinese, or at least by remaining neutral in the conflict, the Romanians have not, in any meaningful sense, allied themselves with China, as have the Albanians. They have simply played astutely on Soviet vulnerabilities. Romania demonstrated its new spirit openly in November 1963, breaking Eastern bloc solidarity by voting in the United Nations for a proposal to establish a nuclear-free zone in Latin America—the first of numerous occasions in recent years when the country has voted against or abstained from supporting Soviet proposals in international bodies. There has also been a new rapprochement with Tito. The Yugoslavs and Romanians have agreed to build one of Europe's biggest hydroelectric and navigation-control projects. Situated on the boundary between the two countries on the Danube's Iron Gate gorge, the project will have cost some $400 million by the time of its scheduled completion in 1971. Significantly, the Romanians have embarked upon the undertaking without any reference to Comecon. The Iron Gate project reflects the Romanian conviction that East-West trade will increase and that Yugoslav-Romanian amity will be lasting.

Despite the Romanian movement toward a closer economic relationship with the West, there has been no ostentatious de-Stalinization operation at work. However, the quality of Romanian political and social life is less zealously narrow-minded than it was in the 1950s. In industrial management, Party hacks are being replaced by trained administrators wherever they are available. Moreover, there is nothing left in the country of classical Stalinism—least of all, what Marxists call the cult of personality. The Romanian leaders today are a true collectivity; the Party leader, Nicolae Ceausescu, presides but does not dictate. When he strikes a pose of independence at international Communist gatherings, or even goes so far as to raise by implication the question of Bessarabia (the Romanian-speaking province ceded under duress to Russia after World War II), presumably he speaks for nearly all his colleagues. And, what is truly significant, he speaks for the vast majority of the Romanian people.

If life in Romania does not have the easygoing affluence of neighboring Yugoslavia, it far surpasses in the amenities the best the Soviet Union is likely to be able to offer for years to come. The story is told that at a party in Bucharest during a recent international medical congress, a Soviet doctor accosted an American. "Tell me, sir," the Russian demanded, with a boldness supplied by several vodkas,

---

VARIOUS SPELLINGS OF "ROMANIA"

There is considerable disagreement over the spelling of "Romania." "Roumania," which is sometimes seen in English, is the French spelling. The spelling "Rumania" is generally used elsewhere in Europe. The Romanians themselves, however, favor the "o" spelling to point out that they are not Slavs, like their neighbors, and to imply that they are descendants of the Roman conquerors of Transylvania and the Dacians, the original inhabitants of the area. Hungarians, who long quarreled with Romania over Transylvania, maintain that the Dacians were killed by the Romans, and that any possible survivors withdrew with the Romans in the Third Century before barbarian onslaughts.

"do you not think we Russians will soon overtake the United States in living standards?"

"Well," answered the American, more adroit at this sort of repartee than is sometimes the case, "it seems to me, sir, that you'll have to overtake the Romanians first."

The Russian, so the report goes, flushed; the American chortled, and—this is the point of the story—the Romanians chortled too.

They had good reason for laughter. The plain truth is that the Soviets will have to run hard and far to catch up with their satellite. Bucharest may not be Belgrade today, but it is all a matter of the angle of approach. Landing at Bucharest airport en route to Western Europe from Moscow can be an exhilarating experience: the city, by contrast to Moscow, is all verve, luxury and socialist *Gemütlichkeit*. The girls are slim and pretty, and they seem to be well dressed until, closer up, the somewhat shoddy quality of the fabrics shows. The movie houses on the main thoroughfares are a good deal more likely to be showing an Italian or French film than a Soviet girl-loves-tractor, boy-loves-tractor romance—and the audiences watching the films imported from the West will certainly be larger and happier.

BUCHAREST'S hotels play host to Japanese, Swedish and Italian trade delegations. Members of the industrial bureaucracy proudly display their new Western-made machine tools and willingly comment on Soviet failures to compete. There are literally hundreds of Western engineers employed throughout the country; Soviet technicians in Romania these days are few. On Romania's Black Sea coast, the Government has established a glittering socialist vacation spa in the town of Mamaia—a kind of season-long Mardi Gras for Swedes, Belgians, Britons, Frenchmen and West Germans searching out a cut-rate holiday in the sun. There, it is not unusual to see Romanians talking with visitors.

This is not to claim that Romania is on the eve of a political millennium. The Romanian police are still clearly in evidence—a potential source of grief for the unwary and a little unnerving in that they are, these days, somewhat unpredictable. Still—and this is the test—there is some hope abroad once again in Romania. Only a few short years ago, Romania was a terror-ridden, dismal country. On summer evenings in Bucharest these days, there are plenty of smiles.

SOUTHWARD, the uneasy Bulgarians wait with increasing impatience for the Soviets to reward their loyalty. Poor and primitive, Bulgaria is the only remaining Russian satellite whose living standard makes that of Russia seem advanced. Occasional murmurings of protest are voiced, particularly over the unhappy fact that huge amounts of the country's best agricultural products—tobacco, fresh fruit and vegetables—are exported to Russia while Bulgarians must content themselves with second-grade produce. Nevertheless, Bulgarian policy remains in most important respects a carbon copy of Moscow's; Bulgaria remains docile—faithful, perhaps, to the nation's traditional attachment to Russia.

Yet, as elsewhere in the once monolithic Soviet bloc, life is easing. True, it is still possible to be sentenced to up to five years of forced labor in Bulgaria for leading "an idle, parasitic way of life." But it is also possible for the first time since World War II to complain, cautiously, about shortages and poor living conditions. From time to time, satirists are even emboldened to poke fun at the Government in the cabarets of Sofia—until the authorities, feeling that matters have gone a bit too far, clamp down again. In the capital one sees an increasing number of Western businessmen who have come to negotiate contracts with Bulgarian Government officials; there are more foreigners in evidence generally (visas are no longer required of tourists); and the Bulgarians themselves appear better dressed than heretofore.

Nevertheless, life improves only slowly—and, since the natural resources at the disposal of Romania are lacking, Bulgaria's prospects for drastic improvement appear remote.

ATTENTIVE GROUP of Romanian Pioneers, the Party-controlled children's organization, watches a teacher paint a doll's head. They attend classes in a former royal palace in Bucharest.

DISPLAY FORMATION of young Bulgarian gymnasts *(opposite)* holds banners aloft at a sports festival in Sofia. Athletes from both sides of the Iron Curtain participated in the event.

A Straitjacket Society Slowly Easing Its Bonds

The trappings of socialist life appear as frequently in the Balkans as in Russia. Youth organizations instruct children in Marxist dogma. Public transportation displays slogans urging workers to exceed their quotas. Nevertheless, the de-Stalinization which has improved conditions for the average citizen in Russia has also taken effect in the Balkans. All of the nations of the peninsula except Albania—which remains grimly totalitarian—are seeking more independence and freedom. Trade with Western Europe and America is creating contacts with democratic attitudes. And a "workers' utopia" like Velenje in Yugoslavia offers living facilities which are superior to anything the Balkan worker or peasant has ever seen.

A PLANNED UTOPIA in Yugoslavia is a showplace of ideal living conditions

INDUSTRIAL COMMUNITY of Velenje in Slovenia is a model town which the Yugoslav Government began to build in 1953. Eventually there will be 35,000 inhabitants in the tall, terraced apartments. The town was planned for coal miners who work in the nearby lignite mine. Separating the new town from the old *(foreground)* are small plots of carefully manicured farmland.

113

NEW HOUSING *offers attractive quarters and modern, streamlined facilities for families*

PRIVILEGED FAMILY, a miner and his two children—their mother is at work—sit at a new table in their apartment *(right)* in Velenje, the model city in Yugoslavia.

HIGH-RISE HOMES in Bucharest tower above workers repairing trolley tracks *(opposite)*. Many of the city's new residences are going up on the outskirts of town.

EVENING RECREATION is open to all at the Workers' Club in Velenje *(below)*. Operating until after midnight, the club offers soft drinks, snacks and television.

NEIGHBORHOOD DANCE, winding through the streets of a suburb of Sofia, Bulgaria, celebrates a local girl's wedding. All the neighbors—even strangers—joined the line of dancers.

ATTENTIVE GUEST links arms with the new bride. The handkerchief he is holding is part of the dance. The wedding itself took place that morning in a Government bureau in Sofia.

THRESHOLD CEREMONY takes place as the bride carries into her new home a loaf of bread topped with a rose. The bridegroom, standing next to her, holds a glass of red wine.

PREPARING THE SUPPER with the other women in the kitchen, the bride takes her turn stirring soup. The guests provided much of the food for the gigantic meal, which lasted all evening and continued into the small hours of the following day.

COLLECTING GIFTS, a well-wisher passes the customary piece of bread on which the guests place money as a token of affection for the newlyweds. Each guest not only gave money but also offered to sing or dance in honor of the wedding couple.

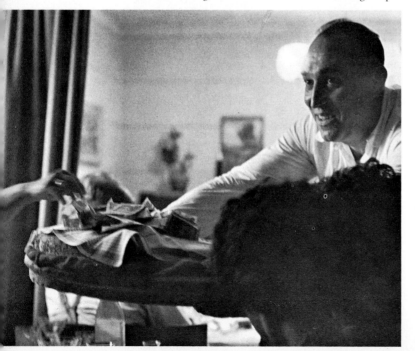

TEARING THE BREAD, the bride rips off the larger half of the loaf in a tug of war with her husband, establishing that she will be the head of the household: by tradition, whoever

tears the bigger piece will rule the home. The reception meal, though abundant, consisted of simple foods such as a meat soup, cucumber salad, meat with potatoes, pudding, slices of the wedding bread, tea and plum brandy. At the end of the party the bride presented each guest with a gift (to one she gave an embroidered tablecloth) and kissed everyone goodbye.

In a stone relief at Split, Yugoslavia, a Croatian king (right) receives a prostrate subject (bottom). The work is from the 10th Century,

when Croatia became a power controlling the Dalmatian coast.

An Other-Worldly Vision

"WHAT news from Europe?" Balkan peasants will ask the stranger who comes among them, expressing in this artless question a sense of difference—an instinctive understanding that they inhabit an emotional dimension, a universe of discourse, alien to our own.

They are right, of course. Geographical links notwithstanding, the Balkans are not European. They are—or were until this century—a separate part of the continent. The Balkans are more closely bound to the Byzantine—the East Roman—world: a world which a thousand years ago dedicated itself to the unearthly and the spiritual.

If the Balkans throughout most of history have been an unlucky place—one of poverty, disease, war, vendetta and political oppression—they have also been a strangely impressive monument to the spiritual powers of man. The region convincingly demonstrates what a materialist age like the 20th Century has too often misunderstood: that true pride and true

121

strength are not at all the same thing as wealth or happiness. This lesson is not quite forgotten in the Balkans. Even today, the old art and literature are still close to the hearts of the people, and in their essence many of these works are variations on a single theme—the expression of contempt for the sufferings of the flesh.

To Westerners, the frequently found Balkan infatuation with suffering, the belief that pride —national and personal—may find its truest expression in defeat, seems so irrational as to be false. No doubt it has its elements of pose and falsity. It is nevertheless a belief which can be found nearly everywhere in the Balkans. It is shared by contradictory elements—by peasant and commissar, by disparate peoples like the Serbs and the Croats, by emotional opposites like the city intellectual and the poor village priest. Pride amidst defeat is the emotional position most admired; a quixotic honor, even at a terribly bloody price, or a stoic acceptance of death, is believed to be the fundamental test of a man. So powerful is this tradition that defeat is a role which the Balkan nations have often consciously seemed to seek (consider the uprising in Belgrade in 1941, which was followed by Nazi Germany's savage retribution on the Yugoslavs). The tradition may in fact help to explain the repeated tragedies which have befallen the Balkans throughout their tortured history.

THIS interest in self-destruction—and a concurrent concern with the things of the spirit and not the flesh—is nowhere plainer than among the Serbs, those quintessential Balkan highlanders. In their folklore, art and poetry they continue to celebrate the inner world rather than the outer. The ultimate paradox is that the Serbs, the most nationalistic of peoples, celebrate not the rise of their nation but its fall.

Every Serb knows the traditional folk epics of his people. They are constantly on his lips. The folklore and ballads of their own ancestors are equally as familiar to Bosnian Moslems,

Albanians, Bulgarians and Romanians. Until the beginning of World War II, every Serbian village festival was the occasion of a solemn recitation. Wandering singers, in the old bardic tradition of Homer, would play the gusle, a one-string, guitarlike instrument, and chant the ancient epics and ballads: those of the cruel 15th Century Queen Jerena, who drove the peasants to build the fortress of Smerderevo; of the necessity of entombing the wife of a nobleman alive in the walls of the city of Scutari in order to appease a nearby mountain spirit; above all, of the saintly Czar Lazar, who spurned earthly glory and suffered defeat for himself, his men and his kingdom. In Rebecca West's celebrated 1941 book on the Balkans, *Black Lamb and Grey Falcon*, the old ballad runs:

> *There flies a grey bird, a falcon,*
> *From Jerusalem the holy . . .*

It is the eve of the tragic battle of Kosovo, and Lazar must make his choice.

> *There is no falcon, no grey bird,*
> *But it is the Saint Elijah.*
> *He carries no swallow,*
> *But a book from the Mother of God.*
> *He comes to the Tsar at Kossovo,*
> *He lays the book on the Tsar's knees.*
> *This book without like told the Tsar:*
> *"Tsar Lazar, of honourable stock,*
> *Of what kind will you have your kingdom?*
> *Do you want a heavenly kingdom?*
> *Do you want an earthly kingdom?"*

The choice is cruel. If Lazar seeks victory—which "lasts only a little time"—he has only to ride out with his cavalry against the Turks, and the Turks will be destroyed. But if he seeks a heavenly kingdom, he must do so at the price of his own death and the defeat of his soldiers. "Build you a church on Kossovo," the ballad goes on. "Build it not with a floor of marble, / but lay down silk and scarlet on the ground . . . / For all your soldiers shall be destroyed, / And you, prince, you shall be destroyed with them." For Lazar, the choice is clear:

Then the Turks overwhelmed Lazar,
And the Tsar Lazar was destroyed,
And his army was destroyed with him,
Of seven and seventy thousand soldiers.

All was holy, all was honourable
And the goodness of God was fulfilled.

To Western ears, all this is quaint and improbable. Rebecca West denounced the old legend: "Lazar was wrong, he saved his soul and there followed five hundred years when no man on these plains, nor anywhere else in Europe for hundreds of miles in any direction, was allowed to keep his soul. . . ."

But preoccupation with the soul and defeat has in no sense caused a failure of nerve in the Balkans. The old epics and ballads have not robbed the Balkan nations of the will to fight —as invaders have learned to their sorrow again and again. The urge to battle against insuperable odds runs through the history of the Balkans, and its nations regularly have acted upon that urge. That will to struggle makes comprehensible the history of the region—from its defiance of the Ottoman Turks to its defiance of the Soviet Union.

The acceptance of tragedy is not limited to the Serbs. In a hauntingly beautiful Romanian ballad, "Miorița," or "The Lamb," a shepherd boy hears evil companions plotting his death. He tells his favorite lamb:

If I'm going to die
In a field of sweet-smelling grass
Tell them to bury me
Near here
In the sheep-fold,
So I may be with you still,
At the back of the sheep-pen
To hear my dogs—
That much tell them.
And at my head you should put
A flute of beech,
Which plays affectionately,
A flute of bone,
Which plays nostalgically,
A flute of elder,

Which has a fiery tone.
When the wind blows
It will pass through them;
The sheep will gather
And will cry blood-tears.
But you shouldn't tell them about the murder.
Tell them
That I got married
To a beautiful queen:
The world's bride;
That at my wedding
A star fell;
The sun and the moon held my crown;
Fir trees and maple trees
Were my wedding guests,
Priests, the big mountains,
Players, birds—
Thousands of birds and star-torches!

Such poetry is the essence of the Balkan spirit, and ancient ballads like "Miorița" are still heard in the Balkan countryside. The old Balkan literature remains a living thing—and is therefore impressive. Regrettably, since the quality of poetry is difficult to convey from one language to another, the Balkan epics— a true expression of pride through the centuries of poverty, degradation and alien rule—are little known beyond their native countries.

More universal by far in its appeal is the language of the Balkan visual tradition—the churches with their frescoes and icons which comprised the arts of the peninsula for hundreds of years before the coming of the Turks in the 15th Century. Even after the Turkish conquest this powerful and uncompromising celebration of the spirit lived on, although only dimly, in the monasteries of the area.

The tradition has endured to this day. Socialist Realism—the vulgar, sermonizing political poster art which the Soviets imported into the Balkans after World War II—has not been strong enough to destroy it. Today, as the national traditions of the Balkan peoples once more revive and make themselves felt in opposition to alien and sterile Soviet political and cultural doctrines, the old style influences even the self-consciously modern artists of Yugoslavia and Romania, who often display themes and symbols derived from the ancient national past. In Yugoslavia, a contemporary painter like Lazar Vujaklija consciously employs the curious symbols of the Bogomil tombs of Bosnia-Hercegovina; the mosaicist Marij Pregelj presents a two-dimensional schematic simplicity which is clearly related to the old Byzantine tradition.

THERE is much of the old tradition worthy of preservation. How much is only now becoming apparent, although the arts came very early to the Balkans. The museums of Yugoslavia, Bulgaria and Romania amply document the first crude artistic explorations of Neolithic man in the Balkan peninsula. But little of this work attains the level of art. One of the earliest examples of fine art in the Balkans is the great Thracian tomb at Kazanluk in central Bulgaria. The tomb is a treasure trove, furnished with exquisite offerings to the dead. The walls are painted with a masterful and sophisticated fresco technique. It is, however, a monument almost entirely derived from Classical Greek art. There are few native Thracian stylistic elements perceptible at Kazanluk. The tomb demonstrates only the power of the Greek idea far beyond Greece itself, as do the votive offerings and carved funereal steles of towns on the Black Sea coasts, or the coins minted by the princelings of the ancient Balkans.

But native elements do appear in the city-states planted by the Greeks and Romans on the Balkan coasts. Archeological excavations of these cities frequently yield up indigenous Balkan art work—steles showing Dacian gladiators, friezes containing Thracian designs, and most of all, the enigmatic figure of the Thracian Horseman, a rider mounted on a prancing steed. The Horseman seems to have been a god of the Danubian Balkan peoples. His effigy is dug up everywhere, in the village fields where the old burial mounds bake in the summer sun, in the dusty sites of the buried Greek and Roman cities, in the ruins of the fortresses of the hill chieftains who carried on a constant guerrilla warfare against the Greek and Macedonian invaders.

The Roman conquest strengthened the Classical tradition in the Balkans. But with the fall of Western Roman power in the peninsula the cultural influence of Byzantium, as the Eastern Roman Empire came to be called, grew to overwhelming proportions. The barbarian invasions which destroyed Roman power in the region uprooted the old life. Once order was restored, the pagan peoples of the peninsula took their culture from the nearest—and most powerful—source at hand. Thus the Balkans—like Russia to the northeast—became part of the world of the Byzantine vision; they cannot be understood unless we make the effort of will to pierce this uncompromising, brilliant, but essentially alien imagination.

THE Byzantine imagination is alien to our own because it is a fusion of two diverse traditions—the Greco-Roman Classical and the Eastern—only one of which we in the Western world truly share. Our civilization and Byzantium's ultimately derive from the Classical world of the Greeks and the Romans, especially as this world received the stamp of Christianity. But in the Fourth Century A.D., the Roman Empire was divided in two—the Western Empire soon to fall before the onslaught of the barbarians who battered at its frontiers, the Eastern to grow mighty and stand as a monument to tenacity and pride for more than a thousand years.

This Eastern Empire was only nominally Roman. Its official language was Latin; its spoken language was Greek. But the Empire was not Grecian. It consisted of a racial and cultural amalgam of Greeks, Anatolians, Syrians, Coptic Egyptians, Armenians and Slavs, together with myriad peoples of Central Asia who drifted into its domain through the porous northeastern frontiers. In the Seventh Century, the Moslem conquest of much of the Mediterranean basin largely cut off Western Europe from Eastern influences. Byzantium, although it lost

North Africa, Egypt and Syria, maintained itself in what are today Turkey, Southern Italy and areas of the Balkans.

For Byzantium, ties with lands farther to the east became strong. The Syrian and Iranian worlds, and beyond these the world of far-off India, radiated their influences on the imperial capital, Constantinople—a city which in the Middle Ages was a meeting place of Europe and Asia, a gorgeous metropolis, rich and dazzling. And Byzantine art, legend and religion reflected these influences, too. The Buddha made an early appearance in Europe in Byzantine dress, together with many heroes of Oriental romances. The Bodhisattva Sakyamuni, an incarnation of the Buddha, appears in the Byzantine legend of *Barlaam and Josaphat* as one Joasaph; he was Budasef and then Judasef in the course of the wanderings of the fable from India to Arabia to the Caucasus and finally to Greece. (He appears in the Middle Ages as St. Josafat, enjoying a church dedicated to him at Palermo, in Sicily.) And what was true of legend was equally true of thought and artistic style in addition.

Byzantine art emerges into the full light of history in the Sixth and Seventh Centuries. Monuments dating from those centuries appear as far afield from Constantinople as Ravenna in the northeast of Italy and Poreč in Istria—both Byzantine beachheads. They reflect an art which had broken with the classical Roman tradition of realism. It was already a contorted art, other-worldly in its interests. Form had become arbitrary and expressionistic: the eyes in the religious paintings stare at us with a

PRIMITIVE STYLE of a painting by the Yugoslav artist Lazar Vujaklija, showing a noble and his heir with hands raised in supplication, takes its inspiration from the tomb carvings of the Bogomils, a religious sect in the Balkans in the Middle Ages.

power designed to impress. They engage the eye of the beholder, attempting to create a mystic bond between the observer and the reality of the inner world which lies behind the image.

A complex symbolism developed, embracing such figures as Christ Pantokrator (the All-Ruler); Christ Evergetes (the Benefactor); the Mother of God in her manifold roles; the glittering warrior saints and archangels and their cohorts organized in the angelic battalions of Thrones, Powers and Dominions; the myriad Old Testament prophets; saints in paradise and sinners in hell.

There were individual modes and symbols appropriate to each. Colors were controlled according to a strict canon. To Christ, writes André Grabar, a French art historian, "pertained blue and cherry-red, sometimes picked out with gold; to the Virgin, all shades of blue; to St. Peter, yellow and light blue; to St. Paul, blue and claret-red; to Emmanuel-Logos, yellow streaked with gold." What was sought after was not originality of expression but a deep and long-tested harmony, expressing the felt truth of another world.

The art traditional to the West for the past 500 years—that is, since the early Italian Renaissance—is something quite different. It is a representational art, one that weds an enormous sophistication of technique to a habit of scientific observation and an intense curiosity about the physical world. Like the Greeks before them, the artists of the Western tradition have exalted the flesh and delighted in the sensuous

125

THE SWIFTLY MOVING BALKAN DANCES

No livelier folk-art form exists than that of the enormously variegated, swiftly moving dances of the Balkans. Like the enduring epics and arts of the region, the dances reflect both the heroism of the Balkan peoples and their efforts to pursue their own ways through troubled centuries. Below are some examples.

WARRIOR DANCES: In the Rusalija of Yugoslavia, men sweep their swords in great arcs as they leap and twist in the constantly shifting *kolo*, or circle, characteristic of most Balkan dances. The eerie sound made by the flashing swords, known as "whiffling," was originally intended to frighten away the beasts of the Balkan forests. The male dancers of the fast-paced Yugoslav *Aramiska*, who brandish swords and pistols, recall a later affliction: the tyranny of 19th Century Turkish provincial governors, who were fought by *Aramis*, or outlaw bands.

SILENT DANCES: Prenuptial dances like the intricate *Vrliko Kolo* of northern Dalmatia are performed without accompaniment in almost total silence, a reminder of feudal days when local lords often took a fancy to nubile peasant girls.

PROPITIATORY DANCES: Led sometimes by men and sometimes by women, these dances call for blessings —for marriage, for fertility, for harvests. One of the oldest of them, today performed solely in the small southern Bulgarian village of Boulgari, is the *Nastinar*, or fire dance, in which the villagers dance barefooted and unharmed on glowing embers each June to ask the assistance of Saints Constantine and Helen in the forthcoming year.

details of the human form and the rich blessings of the material universe. It is a happier and more self-confident vision, but it is not the Byzantine—and Balkan—mode.

Byzantine art in its essence is expressionist, antirealist, symbolic: it is, for one thing, primarily two-dimensional. The tortured saints, the glittering angels with flamelike wings, the grieving apostles who inhabit the magical silence of these wall mosaics, frescoes and icons dwell in an airless space. Their spiritual substance is illuminated against a featureless, flat, golden background that places them in a kind of timeless void—so that their glory, their passions and their suffering are depicted for us in a universal environment, one independent of the accident of place and time. Byzantine art, in later centuries, was to become more humanistic and to pay increasing attention to

the expression of emotion. Yet it was never to lose its basic concern with the world of the spirit.

There is no better expression of the longstanding Byzantine contempt for the envelope of flesh which the ascetic tradition of the Eastern Church urges us to despise than the actual church structures of the Orthodox East. These are, in their original expression in medieval times —in Northern Italy, Istria, Dalmatia, Macedonia and Greece—relatively unadorned structures of brick arranged in geometric patterns on the outside; within, they are something else. Once inside these churches a world of immense richness opens before us. The churches are dark and magical; the altar, in contrast to Western practice, is partially hidden from view. But virtually every inch of space within the holy place is covered with glowing frescoes and icons.

ACCORDING to a scarcely altered tradition which endured intact for nearly a thousand years, walls, domed apses and altar screens are covered with an unworldly, scarcely believable richness of symbol: God in mercy, God in agony, grieving Marys, sinners, innocent Adams, sinning Eves, hell fire, paradise and the blessed legion of saints—the last bespeaking by the eerie greenish glow of flesh the tyranny of corruption over mortal man. For the eye adjusted to this vision, there is hardly an art anywhere so moving. It is not an exaggeration to say that once we enter this world of spirituality, the 500 years of Western art between the Renaissance and the Post-Impressionists of the late 19th Century seem almost a willful detour from what is pure, controlled, self-denying and great. Such, at least, is what more than one modern art critic would say. And if this be an exaggeration, the thought remains as a measure of the achievement of the nameless masters of the Byzantine world between the Sixth and 15th Centuries.

Such an uncompromising and austere artistic vision was peculiarly appealing to the peoples of the Balkans. They took to the style in the

Middle Ages and have not yet truly abandoned it—for all the damage which modernism and the heavy-handed political doctrine of Socialist Realism have worked in our day. But it would be petty chauvinism—regionalism at its most naïve—for the Balkans to claim more than a part in this great esthetic vision. The Balkan masters throughout the thousand years that the tradition was a living thing played no more than an honorable contributing role; one doubts that they would have asked for more recognition than to say that they belonged, with whatever private excellence, to a tradition which was greater than they.

IT was not an age, a culture or an art that encouraged individuality. It urged instead a sense of social solidarity, a pride of craft, a love and skill given in full measure. A French eyewitness who watched the decoration of a monastery church on Mount Athos in Greece in the 19th Century, long after the Byzantine-Slavic tradition had passed its zenith, recorded the details of an operation which cannot have been very different centuries before, and nothing could be further removed from our own cult of the individual artist's personality:

"A young monk," he wrote, "spread the mortar, the master sketched the subject, the first pupil filled in the colours within the outline in the subjects which the master had not time to finish, a young pupil gilded the nimbi, painted inscriptions and made ornaments, two others, smaller, ground and mixed colours. In an hour he drew a picture representing Jesus Christ giving His Apostles the mission of evangelizing and baptizing the world. The Christ and the eleven other personages were nearly life size. He made his sketch from memory without cartoon, drawing or model. . . . His memory was prodigious. He dictated to the second pupil the inscriptions without book or notes, and they were the same as I had seen elsewhere. . . . When the lime was almost dry they finished by adding gold and silver to the dresses, and the finer colours are added—especially Venetian blue—[as well as]

flowers and ornaments . . . it being unnecessary for the lower colours to be dry lest they should soil. Another painter does the lettering and all is finished."

Thus did Balkan artists throughout the years of the living tradition glorify their God and their craft.

Their monuments are there to see. In Macedonia stand the great churches of Nerezi (near Skopje, the capital of modern Macedonia) and nearby Lake Ohrid. North of these in Serbia and in the Raška area—the heartland of the medieval Serbian empire—are the great monastery churches built by the Serbian kings of the Nemanjić line. In Bulgaria, on the outskirts of Sofia, is the little church of Boyanna —and within are glowing 13th Century frescoes worthy to stand with the works of the precursors of the Italian Renaissance.

What underlies this Balkan art in contrast to the pure Byzantine idiom is a somewhat greater sense of humanity—a softening of the bleak intellectualism which is the uncompromising feature of most East Roman art. The Balkan painters worked far from Byzantium, but their art, which is only now being discovered and properly appreciated in the West, has little about it of the provincial in the depreciative sense. The Balkan artists seem not to have lagged behind Constantinople in technique, and surely not in psychological penetration. But they differed in their less austere dedication to the ideal.

WE may be grateful to them. In the remote Balkan mountain valleys, these nameless men labored and worked out an honorable destiny. Spurning everything that suggests the facile, tawdry or cheap, they limned for us a world of inner spirit.

It is a tragic and heroic vision they recorded. There is little in these glowing frescoes which, like the Italian or Flemish art which was shortly to follow theirs, suggests a celebration of life, world and flesh. It is an other-worldly vision. But what they sought to teach us, the world would do well to learn again.

AVANT-GARDE PLAYWRIGHT Eugène Ionesco left Romania just before World War II and settled in Paris. His most famous contribution to the theater is the comedy *Rhinoceros*.

An Expression
of Two Civilizations

Artistic activity in the Balkans during the 20th Century has derived its inspiration from two sources: Paris and Byzantium. Most of what is new and experimental in Balkan art owes at least some of its verve to the French cultural capital. Many Romanians, conscious of their Latin language and affinities, have gone to Paris to work, and the creations of Eugène Ionesco, Georges Enesco and Constantin Brancusi bear a Gallic stamp. Other Balkan artists, however, have expressed the spirit which emanates from the Byzantine Empire. Although Byzantine art was an amalgam of Eastern and Hellenistic cultural traditions, it nevertheless achieved a distinctive quality of its own which is still capable of firing contemporary imaginations.

ROMANTIC COMPOSER Georges Enesco, who died in 1955, is considered Romania's greatest musician. A teacher and a concert violinist, he is known for his *Romanian Rhapsodies.*

NOBEL LAUREATE, Yugoslav novelist Ivo Andrić receives the Nobel Prize *(left)* from Sweden's King Gustav VI in 1961. The award cited *The Bridge on the Drina,* Andrić's epic novel.

STYLIZED ART, whether abstract or religious, expresses a tranquil solemnity

CONTROVERSIAL RECLUSE, the Romanian sculptor Constantin Brancusi created his simple, archetypal images in his Paris studio for 50 years before his death in 1957.

ORTHODOX ICON, *The Savior,* a late 13th Century painting from Macedonia *(opposite),* is typical of the Slavic rendering of religious subjects in the style of Byzantine masters.

RELIGIOUS SCULPTOR, Yugoslavia's Ivan Meštrović *(left),* who died in 1962, sits before a bas relief which reflects, like most of his work, a strong Byzantine influence.

AUSTERITY *of the past is revealed in restored medieval paintings, long hidden under soot and whitewash*

ARMS UPLIFTED reverently, the Virgin Mary adorns a vaulted wall of the Church of St. Clement's in Ohrid, Yugoslavia. Below her is a double scene of Christ administering Communion to His apostles, giving them the bread *(left)* and wine *(right)*. Orthodox Church fathers line the wall below Christ; Biblical figures decorate the arch.

132

THE RILA MONASTERY, a Bulgarian landmark built mostly in the 19th Century, is an attempt to re-create 14th Century Balkan architecture. Many of its 173 rooms, once living quarters for monks, are now hotel accommodations for travelers.

Obstacles to Harmony

IN the Balkans, the imprint of the past is everywhere; the tenacity of the historic imagination in the region can be truly staggering. Rebuke a Bulgarian Communist Party functionary because the electric power fails in the capital's main hotel and he will retort angrily: "We were under the Turks for 500 years!"

In remote areas of Yugoslavia, village women wear metal ornaments very much like those to be found in local graves dating back centuries. The sunburst ornamental motif may be a direct remembrance of the pagan sun cults of pre-Slavic times. Still another remembrance, some say, is the traditional village dance of the Balkans, the *hora* or *horo*, as it is known, respectively, in Romania and Bulgaria, or the *kolo*, as it is known in Yugoslavia. No wedding feast, saint's day or national holiday is considered complete without its impassioned *horo*—danced interminably for hour after hour, long into the night, to the sound of drums and flutes.

Some village embroideries—each village has its traditional motif—may be still older than the *horo*. The shepherds of Romania preserve a younger memory. They wear the white tunics and leather sandals which the sculptured reliefs of the Column of Trajan in Rome faithfully depict captive Dacians wearing in the Second Century A.D.

The names of heroes out of dim history, like the medieval princeling Marko Kraljević, the Albanian resistance leader Skanderbeg, or even the Emperor Trajan himself, are on every peasant's lips. In Serbia and Montenegro, the great personal religious festival of the year is the *Slava*—the anniversary of the "day of glory" on which the celebrant's clan accepted Christianity centuries ago. On this day the priest blesses the *žito*, a traditional feast dish of sweetened boiled wheat dating from pagan times which is also eaten at the grave of the dead—the latter custom being traceable to pre-Christian funeral feasts. In Yugoslavia, even dedicated Communists proudly observe such customs.

Such a sense of the past is not of itself a harmful thing. But the folk memories and legends and the myths of national origin have too often served as a rationale for the chronic Balkan vice—political atrocity against one's neighbors. In the Balkans, appeals to intolerance have frequently fallen on receptive ears. During the Turkish occupation, for example, the Bulgarians suffered from the rapacity of Greek officials employed by the Turks, and from the intolerance of the Greek clergy who used the favored position granted them by the Turks to suppress the native Slavic liturgies and clergy. The Bulgarians did not forget. During World War II, they in turn inflicted unspeakable cruelties on the Greek-speaking villagers of Macedonia and Thrace, regions which had been allotted to them by Hitler.

THE Romanians, too, have been among the most intolerant of peoples. After World War I, they practiced so thoroughgoing and brutal an anti-Semitism that their conduct became an international scandal. And however genuine and praiseworthy today are the continuing efforts of Marshal Tito's regime to administer Yugoslavia as an impartial coalition of the five major peoples—Serbs, Croats, Slovenes, Montenegrins and Macedonians—the hatred between the Orthodox Serbs and the Roman Catholic Croats continues to divide the nation.

Anti-Semitism has not disappeared in Romania; indeed, it remains a kind of endemic disease, increasing as an unfortunate by-product of Romania's struggle against Soviet domination and consequent rediscovery of a national identity. The effect of this native anti-Semitism, however, is limited, since most of Romania's once-large Jewish population emigrated after World War II. More serious is a revival of the discrimination against the long-established Hungarian and German minorities in Transylvania. Never completely assimilated, they have again become targets for pent-up nationalistic frustrations.

IT is doubtful whether social contact between such ethnically kindred peoples as the Serbs and the Bulgarians would be more than minimal, even if a political issue like Titoism did not complicate the picture. A chance meeting between a couple of members of the two groups at a dinner party is likely to resemble an encounter between two stiff and angry alley cats. There has simply been too much suffering and blood on both sides.

Fragmented nationalism has been the besetting curse of the Balkans. But the causes of this destructive nationalism cannot be stated simply. The doctrine of nationalism is by no means native to the Balkans: it grew up in Western Europe in early modern times and first took root in England, Spain and France— countries with well-defined frontiers which had been in existence for centuries before a national consciousness was aroused.

By contrast, the Turkish Empire was a multinational and supranational conception; the Empire did not foster nationalism in the modern Western sense. It followed the millet system: a non-Moslem subject of the Empire belonged to a community determined by his religion— Orthodox, Roman Catholic, Gregorian Armenian, Jewish or Protestant—wherever he might dwell. Nationality depended on religion, not on place or ethnic origin. Such a concept of nationality was ideally suited to the complex mosaic of racial, cultural, religious and linguistic groupings in the Balkans.

As the Empire declined, however, and as the modern doctrine of nationalism struck the Balkans after the French Revolution and the Napoleonic Wars, the millet concept lost force: One land, one folk, became the new cry in the Balkans, as it did in other parts of the continent. Macedonia, for example, was claimed to be *Macedonian:* it belonged to the Slavic-speaking Macedonians of Orthodox faith, and they would kill to make it so. But what of the thousands of Moslems, Jews, Vlachs, Greeks and Albanians who had dwelt in Macedonia for centuries and had as good title as anyone to the land?

In the Habsburg Empire, a similar corrosive process was at work. In the late 19th Century, the subject peoples of the Habsburg Empire began to demand freedom, independence and national union. But how could there be national union in a region like Transylvania or the Banat? Nearly as many Germans and Hungarians dwelt in Transylvania, and Germans and Serbs in the Banat, as did Romanians. The towns were known by two and sometimes three names. The place known as Timişoara in Romanian was Temesvár in Hungarian. Sibiu (Romanian) was Hermannstadt (German) and Nagyszeben (Hungarian). Alba Iulia (Romanian) was Karlsburg (German). While the ideal of a supranational state remained, the discords could be checked. But the new ideas of nationalism shattered the old political structure.

THE Western concept of nationalism in the Balkans resulted in disaster because it was a foreign import that ill-suited the local pattern of life—like so much else that came to backward regions from Western Europe in the 19th and early 20th Centuries. There is no more poignant treatment of this theme than the concluding chapter of *The Bridge on the Drina*—a novel by the Yugoslav writer Ivo Andrić which recounts the story of one town in Bosnia through four centuries of bitter history. In Andrić's account (which won him the Nobel Prize in 1961), the coming of the Austrians in 1878 was an incomprehensible affliction to the Moslems of Bosnia. Equally incomprehensible to the villagers were the incessant activities of the Austrian interlopers—surveyors, engineers and police officials—who totally disturbed the ancient and even tenor of life within the village with their self-important ways and their constant bustle.

What the Austrians were up to— whether they were good or bad—was the interminable subject of gossip and debate. But in 1914, as World War I broke out, the meaning of it all finally became clear after the Austrians dynamited the town bridge—a bridge that had stood for 400 years, ever since the Grand Vizier Mehmet Pasha Sokolović had bequeathed it to the villagers.

Down below . . . was the ruined bridge, horribly, cruelly cut in half. . . . In the distance the pier cut short like a gigantic tree-trunk and scattered in a thousand pieces and the arches to left and right of it brutally cut short. . . . Yes, thought the "hodja" [Moslem priest] more animatedly, for he was now breathing a little more easily, now one can see what all their tools and their equipment really meant, all their hurry and activity. . . . For so many years he had seen how they had always been concerning themselves with the bridge; they had cleaned it, embellished it, repaired it down to its foundations, taken the water supply across it, lit it with electricity, and then one day blown it all into the skies as if it had been some stone in a mountain quarry and not a thing of beauty and value, a bequest. Now one could see what they were and what they wanted. . . . They had begun to attack even the strongest and most lasting of things, to take things away even from God.

Andrić's conclusion is a bitter one:

Perhaps this impure infidel faith that puts everything in order, cleans everything up, repairs and embellishes everything only in order suddenly and violently to demolish and destroy, might spread through the whole world; it might make all of God's world an empty field for its senseless building and criminal destruction. . . . Anything might happen. But one thing could not happen; it could not be that great and wise men of exalted soul who would raise lasting buildings for the love of God, so that the world should be more beautiful and man live in it better and more easily, should everywhere and all for all time vanish from this earth. Should they too vanish, it would mean that the love of God was extinguished and had disappeared from the world. That could not be.

ANDRIC'S spokesman for this creed of love is a Moslem priest. In expressing this credo he is not alone in the Balkans, but he is not entirely typical either. One would like to say that religion and its message of love have been powerful forces for tolerance and understanding in the midst of the bewildering Balkan ethnic kaleidoscope. Alas, this is far from the case. Balkan religion is, after all, Balkan. There, religion instead has become a force for difference, and often for wild hatred.

Least offending in this respect is Islam—an austere creed which preaches, and to some degree practices, the doctrine of the unity of all mankind. But Islam, while still expanding in Africa and Asia, is no longer strong in the Balkans. The decline of Islam is not everywhere a matter of state interference: mosques in Yugoslavia, like churches, function freely. It is that old patterns of existence and ways of thought are disappearing in the modern society that Yugoslavia is in process of becoming.

In Romania, the small Turkish minority which inhabits the Black Sea coast and the Danube delta may not last out this century as a cohesive ethnic and cultural subgroup. The great mosque at Constanţa, built a number of years ago in a vulgar, pseudo-Arabic style by public subscription, is now a museum. Swarms of Russian, Belgian, Czech, East German, French, British and Swedish tourists from the nearby beach resort of Mamaia come to see it; but the mosque functions for the city's Moslem community as

a place of worship only once each week. More than 200,000 Moslems of Turkish extraction were expelled from Bulgaria during the 1950s. In Albania, where 70 per cent of the population is estimated to be Moslem, and where Islam has been savagely persecuted by the Communist regime, few persons practice the faith openly.

Far more resistant to pressure is the Roman Catholic faith. Roman Catholicism is firmly established in western Yugoslavia, which has been faithful to Rome for more than a thousand years. In the Balkans, Roman Catholicism has a passionate intensity: almost every mountain path in Slovenia displays a crucifix, some bearing a larger-than-life representation of Christ in Agony, crowned with thorns, the wounds red with ruby-glass blood. (To come on such a figure for the first time in the eerie Balkan night is one of the psychological hazards of travel in the remoter districts.)

This strong pride in faith appears, too, in the great Baroque churches of Croatia and Slovenia, which were maintained by the peasants throughout the post-World War II persecutions in which priests were jailed and bishops were forbidden to communicate with Rome. The Roman Catholics have survived. The worst furies of persecution in the Balkans have now passed (except in Albania), and the Church has emerged relatively intact.

THE major faith of the Balkans, and the one that in matters of religious doctrine sets the region off from Western Europe, is still the Orthodox Church. (It is not, as many make the mistake of believing, the Greek Orthodox Church. Except in the time of the Turkish occupation, the Balkan churches were independent and national—there were usually, for example, a Serbian Orthodox Church and a Bulgarian Orthodox Church.)

The inner quality of the Orthodox Church is very different from that of the Roman Catholic and Protestant Churches of the West. It is not merely that members of the Orthodox faith cross themselves "backwards"—moving the hand from right to left rather than left to right, as is the Roman Catholic custom—take Communion with leavened bread, or conduct their services in languages native to those who participate in the sacrifice of the Mass. The difference is a compound of two qualities—a greater informality and a greater sense of mystery. As a rule, there are no pews in an Orthodox church: the congregation stands and moves about, coming and going as it chooses, engaging in private prayer, stepping aside for latecomers, leaving in the midst of the celebration of the most solemn offices.

Moreover, an Orthodox church is dark and comparatively intimate. It does not, like a Gothic cathedral in Western Europe, attempt to project the feeling of a linear movement to the altar through alternating bands of light and darkness, symbolizing, as it were, man's life on earth and his procession toward the godhead. The Orthodox church is essentially a square capped by a dome, beneath which all the congregation stands together, while behind the iconostasis—the painted screen that hides the sanctuary and the altar—deep mysteries are played out.

CECIL STEWART, a sympathetic British observer, has noted that in an Orthodox church, "there are no hymns, no instrumental music, only an intimate companionship in which even the singers who chant the offices are not separated, like the Western surpliced choirs, but are members of the congregation amongst whom they stand. The voices reverberate within the church, and, because of the special acoustic properties of the dome, seem to be reflected from the [images of Christ depicted on the dome] and echoed by the heavenly host which surrounds Him. At night, when it is dark, candles flicker in every hand, and above, swinging gently, there is the corona, a suspended circle of lights which by its movement seems to animate the angels and the saints which line the walls and vaults. The divine mysteries are thus, to the initiate, revealed."

In the Orthodox Church the sense of community is everything. It appears in the jocular familiarity displayed by the village priest, who is frequently a married man, as permitted by Orthodox custom. He moves easily and freely among his people. It appears in the holy services, which, since they are conducted in the vernacular, bind clergy and laity together. It is most charmingly revealed at Easter, when after midnight services, the celebrants file outside the church to kiss each other, saying, "Christ is risen," and replying in the traditional words, *"Vaistinu vaskrese!"*—"Risen indeed!" In this simple ceremony the members of the community jointly renew their faith for the entire year.

BUT this sense of community is for Serbs alone, for Bulgarians alone, for Macedonians alone, for Romanians alone. Whatever their manifest virtues, the members of the Orthodox priesthood have sometimes been ignorant and backward—and great stimulators of intolerant strife among the Balkan peoples. The community they love seldom extends beyond the narrow group—which defends its separateness with a fierce pride born of long persecution and national tragedy.

The deadly process does not stop with mere intolerance. For the present, the discords engendered by national and religious differences have been somewhat damped down by the harsh policies of the Balkan Communist regimes which seized power in the troubled years after the last war. But the new political quarrels in the Communist world only partially masquerade older, underlying conflicts of national interest. As Soviet power wanes in the Balkans, the old divisions are appearing once more. We may expect a return of discord—and possibly of mass violence as well.

Today the Soviet effort to impose unity on the Balkans by force is clearly failing. After the disappearance of Communism, whenever that day of deliverance may come, unity will have to be achieved through the free consent of all. But as the bloody experience of the Balkans in this century attests, free consent will be no easy thing to achieve.

SKILLED POTTER, a nun from the Orthodox convent at Agapia, Romania, creates a bowl. Wages which the state pays to the nuns for handicrafts are used to maintain the convent.

Religion's Reluctant Surrender to Force

Religious faiths of all varieties in the Balkans have had their activities severely limited under Communist rule. Official Government attitudes toward the predominant faiths vary according to the political significance of each cult. The Roman Catholics, who are traditionally Western-oriented, have met repeatedly with the most rigorous persecution. The holy orders of Orthodoxy, like the clergy of other sects, must submit to Party regulations—as in the Romanian convent at Agapia shown on these pages. The state has been more lenient with Islam, and Moslem leaders in Yugoslavia and Albania have even served as Government apologists abroad.

STUDENT DORMITORY houses novices at Agapia. Although the Romanian Orthodox Church is allowed to train nuns and priests, the state forbids religious teaching in public schools.

RICH INTERIOR of the church at Agapia *(left)* serves as a quiet setting for a nun reading at a lectern. The convent has several hundred nuns and nearly a hundred acres of farmland.

MUSIC CLASS for seminary students is led by a bearded violinist. Traditionally, the Orthodox Church has cooperated with the state; the nuns elect two delegates to the local People's Council.

MOSLEM MINARET rises above the lighted dome of the Ali Pasha Mosque in the old Bosnian capital of Sarajevo, Yugoslavia. The more than two million Yugoslav Moslems, Europe's largest Islamic group, maintain amicable relations with the state.

ROMAN CATHOLIC CRUCIFIX by the roadside in Slovenia *(left)* is one of many such shrines in northwest Yugoslavia. Although Marshal Tito has tried to discredit Catholicism in Yugoslavia, he has failed to extirpate the people's deep-rooted faith.

ORTHODOX POMP in the Belgrade Cathedral *(opposite)* marks a service for a small congregation. Historically a guardian of Serbian nationalism and the monarchy, the Orthodox Church in Yugoslavia has repeatedly incurred the wrath of the Government.

10

The Passing
of the Old

ON the river embankment in Sarajevo, near the place where Gavrilo Princip stood to assassinate the heir-presumptive to the throne of Austria that fatal day in June 1914, there is a museum. Within are the relics and photographs of the seven youths who plotted murder that summer morning a half century ago and brought a world crashing down. A shabby attendant keeps the little museum. There is a book for visitors' names, but there are few visitors. An inconspicuous tablet in the street marks the place where Princip stood: "Here, in this historic place," the inscription runs, "Gavrilo Princip was the initiator of liberty, on the day of St. Vitus, the 28th day of June 1914."

Few of the passersby who crowd the river embankment stop to read the tablet. Sarajevo today is no torpid Balkan village; no one has time to pause. The tempo of life is swift. For Yugoslavs, caught up in the myriad problems of living, the bullets that struck down an age are ancient history now. On June evenings they promenade the streets in the traditional *korzo* and dance in the nearby cafés; where Franz Ferdinand was shot, one can hear the monstrously amplified twang of electric guitars. The young people are terribly knowing and cynical, little given to heroics or even to belief. The age of Princip's romantic nationalism, only 50 years ago, and the bitter, uncompromising pride which animated the Yugoslav resistance in the last war seem impossibly remote. The freedom Princip died for was won in 1918, compromised in the 1930s, lost again in 1941 and betrayed in 1945. It is only slowly making its return. For the young people of today's Balkans, freedom means not blood but material happiness—a motorcycle, a girl, a private room free of the all-encompassing claims of the political life of the state.

They have learned our vices and they are very modern now in the Balkans. In Split, the old walled city on the Adriatic where 1,700 years ago the Emperor Diocletian built his palace and retired to live out his days, the tourist cabarets in the summer offer a nightly "Festival of Strip." At Niš, the sad old town in the central Balkans where the Emperor Constantine the Great was born, members of the middle-aged Communist bureaucracy—a group Tito's former associate Milovan Djilas has labeled the New Class—take the waters and dance in the magic Balkan evening to the beat of inexpert jazz. In Plovdiv, deep in the heart of the south Bulgarian plain, the collective farmers stand around the Balkantourist Hotel bar, feeding 50-*stotinki* pieces to an extraterrestrial jukebox neatly marked as the product of the Rock-Ola Manufacturing Corporation of Chicago, Illinois.

IT is all changing—and changing fast. The old Balkans—that world of passionate, near-mystical communalism and deeply felt clan loyalties—will not last out the century, not even in the remote mountain enclaves of Albania and Montenegro. Like some hungry plant, Western technology puts down its tendrils everywhere. Tireless work brigades dynamite the mountain passes, blasting roadways through the mountain rock. Tractors and disk harrows churn up the collective fields, scoring deep furrows that violate the old Balkan landscape of patchwork fields. The new fields stretch to the faraway horizon. It is a sight to gladden a Texas heart,

but it is not Balkan. The shepherds are driven each morning to the pastures in buckboard trucks. On the Black Sea coast, the state tourist trusts build glass and prestressed-concrete resort hotels to house the East bloc bureaucrats and myriad Swedish, Belgian, German, French and British clerks and salesmen, all searching out a holiday in the sun. Where the Tatars of the Golden Horde once rode, where the crusaders died, Germans in *Lederhosen* stride about, red-faced, noisy and doggedly healthy. Here the wives of the Communist New Class—women who a decade ago drew water at the village well—posture in ill-chosen bikinis and mingle with the bourgeois West to learn the new arts of supermarket living.

ALL this is a kind of progress, of course, but saddening too. Czar Lazar chose for himself the other-worldly kingdom offered by the prophet Elijah rather than victory over the Turks at the battle of Kosovo on June 28, 1389, but the young people of the Balkans—and their elders—want none of that. They are all weary of tragedy; they are restless, ambitious, hungry for material comforts and ease. It is not easy to blame them, but two things are somehow wrong. The impassioned idealism that drove Gavrilo Princip to the extremity of assassination and the Belgrade citizens to riot in the streets in March 1941, rather than submit to Hitler, seems forever gone. If that sometimes noble passion exists anywhere in the Balkans today, it lives on only as a perversion—in the hard, puritanical Albanian Communism, which espouses a brutal radicalism and a dedicated assertion of independence and difference. The second flaw is a related one: material progress in today's Balkans has not come through any harmonious fusion of the region's past with the insistent demands of the present. It has been bought at the price of political freedom.

This is not to say that the Balkans have been, in the memory of man, a free and happy place. There was much brutality, political caprice and sorrow in the old Balkans. But the dream of freedom existed—and it was real. There was once no Balkan nation which did not aspire to freedom with justice in the best tradition of the Western world. In a more cynical age, that passion has today gone by the board. The Balkan states—once the least rationally calculating of nations, although this is not to say that they were not covetous and greedy—have succumbed to material envy. In today's Balkans the elders serve out their lives, seeking only a little peace, and the young suppress their immaterial longings. All the young people of the modern Balkan states, it seems, want *things*—a material prosperity for which no price seems too high.

Some will not grieve the passing of the old Balkans. It was a brutal place, one of gratuitous death and pointless suffering. But tragic and atrocious as was the past, its brutality was compatible with dignity: suffering and human degradation are not the same at all.

There is no dignity in the efficient authoritarianism and thought-control of the modern police state which rules today's Balkans—and in its worst form, as in Albania, demands not merely compliance but spiritual capitulation and love. The old Balkans were replete with pathos and tragedy. But terrible as the old life was, even in the worst years of the Turks, it cannot be said that the human spirit was utterly crushed, and in the years after the Turkish expulsion, there was, by today's standards, some decent hope of self-expression. If politics then were savage, there was still an ample scope for personality in love of earth, clan, legend and past.

THOSE years were poor ones. Recently the Balkan lands have become richer, but only on a simple scale of values that stresses material accomplishments to the exclusion of all else. In a real sense the old Balkans were no mere backward outpost of Europe but a passionate refusal: an alternative system of life that purposefully exalted other values and other ends.

The Balkans, as an appendage of Europe, are not well understood by European—still less American—imaginations. The Balkan world which emerged from Turkish occupation in the late 19th Century was one which had been cut loose from its roots. In Africa and Asia today the pattern is essentially the same: the folk cultures have been eroded and discredited. The young people are set adrift, the old morality is brought into comic disrepute. All this has happened, moreover, in the midst of a material burgeoning.

THERE has been an ever-deeper penetration of the material civilization of America and Western Europe—but accompanied too by the deadly process of detribalization. This is the sundering of the tribal member from place and past which occurs amid the growth of a vast social anxiety. No werewolves trouble the sleep of today's Balkan peasant sophisticates; the *dracul* is gone. Disappeared, too, are the mountain *vile* and Perun, the thunder god. But hardboiled youths roam the nighttime streets of the Balkan cities, equipped with knives and bicycle chains. And they are rather more likely than the old folk monsters to work physical harm.

The memories of the old years are all faded now. There are a few alive to this day who were haiduks in the mountains, who fought in *komitadžis,* or guerrilla bands, against the Turks for the liberation of Macedonia or the expulsion of the Kaiser's armies from their hills. But the old men are all discredited now. So great is the social cataclysm visited on these regions by World War II and the subsequent invasion of Stalinism that the life that existed before the war can hardly be recalled—even by those who were grown to maturity then, and had made that life, with all its terrible imperfections, what it was.

In Yugoslavia, even the old Partisan irregulars—those who fought in the mountains and woods against the Fascist Ustashi and Nazis and endured hardships impossible to match in the annals of wartime resistance in the West—are all middle-aged and coronary-prone now, many of them bound to desks and goaded to seek ever-higher bonuses by anxious wives who covet fur coats and gleaming new automobiles.

On a Sunday in Kalemegdan, the Belgrade park that houses a museum of the resistance, one can see the ex-heroes pausing in mute wonder before the faded photographs of their past: There they are, in ragged ranks in the snowy woods, clutching captured rifles, un-shaven, dirty, desperate, pitifully weak . . . and terribly brave. The men stand before the me-morials of another time and see themselves as they were in those terrible years so long ago—and they shake their heads and, wordlessly, move on. "Life," as the Slavic peasant says, "is not so simple as crossing a field." Once, no doubt, they believed that the expulsion of the Nazis would solve everything. But the complexities remain, and grow.

It is no good complaining. Industrialism, modernity, material progress—these things are coming now to the old guarded enclaves of the earth—those "backward" lands of which the old Balkans were once the very symbol. If the gifts of the 20th Century come too often garbed in ugly political ideologies, we must remember, of course, that the raw and new are often ugly. It is possible to hope that with the years some more harmonious synthesis of the Balkan past and the hypermodern will emerge.

CERTAINLY Communism—that newest affliction in the Balkan chronicle of afflic-tions—is in flux. One may doubt that Commu-nism, for all its shrill self-assertion, is more than a transitional phase in Yugoslavia. An excellent argument can be offered that Yugo-slav Communism is an unstable synthesis of Eastern and Western elements that will not much outlast the passing of Josip Broz Tito—its architect and greatest pillar. (It might also be suggested that the political and social sys-tem of post-Tito Yugoslavia will not repro-duce the political and social life of the United States or Western Europe.) An evolution of the system may also confidently be expected in Romania, where old ties with Western cul-ture and a sense of ethnic difference from the Russians must, in the long run, weaken such

relations with Moscow as are imposed by the geographical nearness of a powerful neighbor.

The Bulgarian future is less easy to predict. There is a powerful tradition of communalism at work in Bulgarian society—a communalism that dates from the Middle Ages, is perhaps stronger than the related tradition in Serbia, and within living memory found powerful ex-pression in *zadrugas,* communal and patriarchal farming households. There is also a powerful sentimental tie to Russia, whatever political form the Russians may adopt. Yet even in Bulgaria there are Western influences, and ul-timate needs which orthodox Communism can-not supply.

PERHAPS the Albanian future is the dark-est of all. The association with distant Pe-king is baleful. But even here it is important to remember that Albania, as a nation, is very young. What the future holds cannot be meas-ured accurately in this decade.

Mutability—change—is the primary lesson taught by Balkan history. The theme of unpre-dictable change is a constant in the region's past, and no more can the modern Soviets view the future of this area with confidence than could the imperial Turks or Austrians. Precise-ly what events lie ahead no one can foresee, but it is clear that the Russian position has been badly compromised.

Whatever the Soviet role may be 10 years from now, one cannot view the Balkan future without foreboding. It is possible to suspect that the old Balkan demons of violence, pride, anger and passionate waywardness still lurk be-neath the contemporary mask.

The symbol of the Balkans is still the barren Karst, the desolate limestone mountain region, empty of life and hope, which borders the Adriatic Sea. And standing amid this night-mare landscape which is the essence of the tragic Balkan past, one may ask in the words of the prophet Ezekiel the ancient question: "Can these bones live?"

And the answer—now as then—remains: "Lord God, Thou knowest."

A mother and child prepare for a nap in a Romanian village. Next page: Young people dance and drink at Sunny Beach, Bulgaria.

A CRESCENDO OF CHANGE *promising the Balkans an end to suffering . . .*

. . . also threatens to undermine the dignity of the traditionally independent

individual by tempting him with the elusive values of a new, materialistic world

Appendix

HISTORICAL DATES

B.C.

c.1300-750	Indo-European tribes settle on the Balkan peninsula
c.750-500	Greek colonies grow up on the Balkan coasts
357-323	Ascendancy of Macedonian Empire. Most of the peninsula is brought under its control
c. 3rd and 2nd Centuries	Rome brings the Balkan peninsula under its rule

A.D.

330	Constantine transfers the capital of the Roman Empire to Byzantium (later known as Constantinople)
c. 500-700	Slavic tribes migrate into the Balkans
7th-9th Centuries	The first of the Bulgars, an Asian people, take possession of the territory between the Danube and the Balkan mountains
865-870	The Bulgarians become converted to Orthodox Christianity
893-927	The "First" Bulgarian kingdom extends its power from the Adriatic to the Black Sea
10th Century	Serbs accept Orthodoxy and Slovenes and Croats convert to Roman Catholicism
1018	Basil II of the Byzantine Empire annexes Bulgaria
11th Century	Transylvania comes under the control of the Hungarian crown. The Serbs rise against the Byzantine Empire and establish two states: Zeta and Raška
12th Century	Stefan Nemanja unites the Serbs and establishes the base for the future Serbian Kingdom. The Bulgarians rise against Constantinople and found the "Second" Bulgarian Empire
1204	Western forces take Constantinople in the Fourth Crusade
c.1250-1350	Latin-speaking Romanians found the principalities of Walachia and Moldavia
1330	Bulgaria is defeated by Serbia and becomes its vassal
1331-1355	Serbia reaches the height of its power under Stefan Dušan. He doubles the area of his state
1354	Turks establish themselves on European soil at Gallipoli
1389	At the head of a Balkan coalition, the Serbian Czar Lazar attempts to halt the Turkish advance but is defeated at Kosovo. Serbia becomes a vassal

	state of the Turks
1393	The Bulgarian kingdom passes under Ottoman rule
1453	The Turks take Constantinople
1463	The Turks conquer the Slavic kingdom of Bosnia
1468	Albania succumbs to Ottoman rule
1500-1566	The Ottoman Empire attains its height: almost the entire Balkan peninsula is now under its domain
1683	The Turks march on Vienna and are routed
1684-1699	European powers defeat the Turks in the War of the Holy League. The Ottomans lose many of their Balkan holdings
1774	Russia defeats the Turks and is made "guarantor" of Moldavia and Walachia
1799	The Montenegrins succeed in gaining Turkish recognition of their independence
1804-1813	The Serbs under Karageorge unsuccessfully revolt against the Turks
1815-1830	Serbia revolts again and gains autonomy
1829	Russia defeats Turkey again. The Treaty of Adrianople guarantees the autonomy of Moldavia and Walachia, and establishes a Russian protectorate over them
1856	The European powers and Turkey defeat Russia in the Crimean War. Russia relinquishes its protectorate over Moldavia and Walachia, which, along with Serbia, are placed under the powers' collective protection
1859	Moldavia and Walachia are unified and named "Romania"
1875-1877	Insurrections against the Turks break out throughout the Balkans. Russia champions Balkan liberation and, joined by Serbia and Montenegro, declares war on Turkey
1878	The Turks are defeated. Serbia and Romania gain total independence from Turkish rule. Bulgaria wins autonomy. Austria-Hungary is awarded Bosnia and Hercegovina
1885	Active rivalry breaks out between Bulgaria, Serbia and Greece over the Turkish province of Macedonia
1912-1913	The First Balkan War. The Balkan League—Serbia, Bulgaria, Greece and Montenegro—de-

	clares war on Turkey and reduces its European territory to a pocket in the southeastern Balkans. The Albanians revolt against the Turks and proclaim independence
1913	The Balkan League collapses and Serbia and Greece fight Bulgaria. Romania and Turkey enter the war and Bulgaria is forced to cede much territory
1914	The Archduke Franz-Ferdinand is assassinated in Sarajevo
1918-1923	World War I ends and five years of treaty negotiations ensue. The collapse of three empires —the Austro-Hungarian, the Russian and the Turkish—releases vast territories to be divided among the new Balkan states. Romania more than doubles its area; Bulgaria loses territory to Greece and the new state of the South Slavs, which takes over all of Bosnia and Hercegovina and the former Habsburg territories of Croatia and Slovenia
1918	The United Kingdom of the Serbs, Croats and Slovenes, later called Yugoslavia, is formally proclaimed
1925	Albania is proclaimed a republic
1934	Romania, Yugoslavia, Greece and Turkey conclude the Balkan Pact, a mutual nonaggression treaty. King Alexander of Yugoslavia is assassinated
1938	King Carol of Romania establishes a dictatorship
1939	Italy occupies Albania
1939-1944	World War II breaks out. Bulgaria and Romania join the Axis powers. Yugoslavia is occupied. Resistance movements are organized in Yugoslavia and Albania
1944-1946	Romania and Bulgaria are occupied by Soviet troops which oversee the creation of Communist governments. Communist-dominated governments in Yugoslavia and Albania are recognized by the West
1948	Yugoslavia is expelled from the Cominform
1955	Moscow makes overtures of reconciliation to Yugoslavia, which refuses to return to the Soviet orbit
1961	Albania breaks with the Soviets
1962-Present	Balkan nations assert increasing independence from U.S.S.R.

FOR FURTHER READING

CHAPTER 1: LAND AND CHARACTER

Cross, Samuel H., *Slavic Civilization Through the Ages*. Russell & Russell, 1963.

Edwards, Lovett F., *Introducing Yugoslavia*. Methuen, London, 1954.

Halecki, Oscar, *Borderlands of Western Civilization*. Ronald Press, 1952.

Halpern, Joel Martin, *A Serbian Village*. Columbia University Press, 1958.

Jelavich, Charles and Barbara, eds., *The Balkans in Transition*. University of California Press, 1963.

Mylonas, George E., *The Balkan States: An Introduction to Their History*. Eden Publishing House, 1946.

Sanders, Irwin T., *Balkan Village*. University of Kentucky Press, 1949.

Schevill, Ferdinand, *The History of the Balkan Peninsula*. Harcourt, Brace, 1933.

Seton-Watson, Hugh, *The East European Revolution*. Frederick A. Praeger, 1956.

Seton-Watson, R. W., *A History of the Roumanians*. Shoe String Press, 1934.

Stavrianos, L. S., *The Balkans since 1453*. Holt, Rinehart and Winston, 1963.

"Yugoslavia Today: A Special Supplement." *The Atlantic*. Vol. 210, No. 6, December 1962.

CHAPTER 2: VANISHED SPLENDORS

Chekrezi, Constantine, *Albania, Past and Present*. Macmillan, 1919.

Clark, Charles Upson, *Greater Roumania*. Dodd, Mead, 1922.

The Eastern Roman Empire, 717-1453. Vol. 4, *The Cambridge Medieval History*. Macmillan, 1927.

Eliot, Sir Charles, *Turkey in Europe*. Edward Arnold, London, 1908.

Macdermott, Mercia, *A History of Bulgaria, 1393-1885*. George Allen & Unwin, London, 1962.

Miller, William, *The Ottoman Empire and Its Successors*. Cambridge University Press, 1936.

Runciman, Steven, *A History of the First Bulgarian Empire*. G. Bell and Son, London, 1930.

Vasiliev, A. A., *History of the Byzantine Empire*. University of Wisconsin Press, 1953.

CHAPTER 3: CONQUEST, ANARCHY AND WAR

Adams, J. C., *Flight in Winter*. Princeton University Press, 1942.

Cary, Joyce, *Memoir of the Bobotes*. University of Texas Press, 1960.

Fay, Sidney Bradshaw, *The Origins of the World War*. Macmillan, 1948.

May, Arthur J., *The Hapsburg Monarchy, 1867-1914*. Harvard University Press, 1951.

Newman, Bernard, *Albanian Back-Door*. Herbert Jenkins, London, 1936.

Schmitt, Bernadotte E., *The Coming of the War*, 2 vols. Charles Scribner's Sons, 1930.

Stavrianos, L. S., *The Balkans, 1815-1914*. Holt, Rinehart and Winston, 1963.

Taylor, Edmond, *The Fall of the Dynasties*. Doubleday, 1963.

Wolff, Theodor, *The Eve of 1914*. Alfred A. Knopf, 1936.

CHAPTER 4: YEARS BETWEEN THE WARS

Barker, Elisabeth, *Macedonia, Its Place in Balkan Power Politics*. Royal Institute of International Affairs, 1950.

Churchill, Winston, *Triumph and Tragedy*, Vol. 6; *The Second World War*. Houghton Mifflin, 1953.

Hoptner, J. B., *Yugoslavia in Crisis, 1934-1941*. Columbia University Press, 1962.

Kennan, George F., *Russia and the West under Lenin and Stalin*. Little, Brown, 1960.

Marriott, J.A.R., *The Eastern Question, A Study in European Diplomacy*. Oxford University Press, 1940.

Mitrany, David, *The Land and the Peasant in Rumania; The War and Agrarian Reform, 1917-1921*. Yale University Press, 1930.

Pribichevich, Stoyan, *World Without End*. Reynal and Hitchcock, 1939.

Seton-Watson, Hugh, *Eastern Europe between the Wars, 1918-1941*. Cambridge University Press, 1946.

Shirer, William L., *The Rise and Fall of the Third Reich*. Simon & Schuster, 1960.

West, Rebecca, *Black Lamb and Grey Falcon*. Viking Press, 1941.

White, Leigh, *The Long Balkan Night*. Charles Scribner's Sons, 1944.

CHAPTER 5: CHALLENGE TO THE KREMLIN

Bass, Robert and Elizabeth Marbury, *The Soviet-Yugoslav Controversy, 1948-58: A Documentary Record*. Prospect Books, 1959.

Byrnes, Robert F., ed., *Yugoslavia: East-Central Europe under the Communists*. Frederick A. Praeger, 1957.

Dellin, L.A.D., ed., *Bulgaria: East-Central Europe under the Communists*. Frederick A. Praeger, 1957.

Rothschild, Joseph, *The Communist Party of Bulgaria*. Columbia University Press, 1959.

St. John, Robert, *The Silent People Speak*. Doubleday, 1948.

Wolff, Robert Lee, *The Balkans in Our Time*. Harvard University Press, 1956.

CHAPTER 6: YUGOSLAVIA

Armstrong, Hamilton Fish, *Tito and Goliath*. Macmillan, 1951.

Dedijer, Vladimir, *Tito*. Simon & Schuster, 1953.

Djilas, Milovan, *Conversations with Stalin*. Harcourt, Brace & World, 1962. *Anatomy of a Moral*. Frederick A. Praeger, 1959. *Land Without Justice*. Harcourt, Brace, 1958. *The New Class*. Frederick A. Praeger, 1957.

Heppell, Muriel, and Frank B. Singleton, *Yugoslavia*. Frederick A. Praeger, 1961.

Hoffman, George W., and Fred Warner Neal, *Yugoslavia and the New Communism*. Twentieth Century Fund, 1962.

Maclean, Fitzroy, *The Heretic: The Life and Times of Josip Broz-Tito*. Harper & Brothers, 1957.

CHAPTER 7: ALBANIA, BULGARIA, ROMANIA

Cretzianu, Alexandre, ed., *Captive Rumania*. Frederick A. Praeger, 1956.

Fischer-Galati, Stephen, ed., *Romania: East-Central Europe under the Communists*. Frederick A. Praeger, 1957.

Griffith, William E., *Albania and the Sino-Soviet Rift*. M.I.T. Press, 1963.

Hamm, Harry, *Albania*. Frederick A. Praeger, 1963.

Hasluck, Margaret, *The Unwritten Law in Albania*. Cambridge University Press, 1954.

Roberts, Henry L., *Rumania, Political Problems of an Agrarian State*. Yale University Press, 1951.

Skendi, Stavro, ed., *Albania: East-Central Europe under the Communists*. Frederick A. Praeger, 1956.

CHAPTER 8: LITERATURE AND THE ARTS

Bartók, Béla and Albert B. Lord, *Serbo-Croatian Folk Songs*. Columbia University Press, 1951.

Bihalji-Merin, Oto, *Byzantine Frescoes and Icons in Yugoslavia*. Harry N. Abrams, 1958.

Grabar, André, *Byzantine Painting*. Skira, Geneva, 1953.

Hamilton, J. Arnott, *Byzantine Architecture and Decoration*. B. T. Batsford, London, 1933.

Heer, Friederich, *The Medieval World*. Mentor, 1963.

Kadić, Ante, *Contemporary Serbian Literature*. Mouton, The Hague, 1964. *Contemporary Croatian Literature*. Mouton, The Hague, 1960.

Krustev, Kiril, and Vassil Zahariev, *Old Bulgarian Painting*. Bulgarski Houdozhnik, Sofia, 1961.

Pinto, Vivian, ed., *Bulgarian Prose and Verse*. Oxford University Press, 1957.

Rice, David Talbot, *Byzantine Art*. Penguin Books.

Stewart, Cecil, *Serbian Legacy*. Harcourt, Brace, 1959. *Byzantine Legacy*. George Allen & Unwin, London, 1947.

CHAPTER 9: RELIGION AND PEOPLES

Baynes, Norman H., and H. St. L. B. Moss, *Byzantium*. Oxford Paperbacks, 1961.

Benz, Ernst, *The Eastern Orthodox Church*. Anchor Books, 1963.

Durham, Mary Edith, *Some Tribal Origins, Laws, and Customs of the Balkans*. George Allen & Unwin, London, 1928. *High Albania*. Edward Arnold, London, 1908.

Lodge, Olive, *Peasant Life in Jugoslavia*. Seeley, Service, London, 1941.

Runciman, Steven, *The Medieval Manichee*. Viking Press, 1961.

Ware, Timothy, *The Orthodox Church*. Penguin Books, 1963.

Zernov, Nicolas, *Eastern Christendom*. Putnam's Sons, 1961.

FAMOUS BALKAN CULTURAL FIGURES AND THEIR PRINCIPAL WORKS

LITERATURE

Marulić, Marko	1450-1524	Croatian. Epic poetry: *Judita*
Držić, Marin	c.1518-1567	Croatian. Comedies which give a vivid picture of 16th Century Ragusan life
Gundulić, Ivan	c.1589-1638	Croatian. Poetry: *Osman*, an epic in 20 cantos recounting victories over the Turks
Križanić, Juraj	1618-1683	Croatian. Political treatises favoring pan-Slavism
Paisiy, Father	1722-1793	Bulgarian. A history of the Slavic-Bulgarian people which rekindled a national consciousness
Karadžić, Vuk Stefanović	1787-1864	Serbian. Important linguistic reforms and collections of poetry and folktales
Prešeren, France	1800-1849	Slovenian. The founder of modern Slovene literature
Njegoš, Petar Petrović	1813-1851	Prince Bishop of Montenegro. Dramatic poem: *The Mountain Wreath*, describing Montenegro's liberation from the Turks
Mazuranić, Ivan	1814-1890	Croatian. Poetry: *The Death of Smail Aga*
Alecsandri, Vasile	1821-1890	Romanian. Poetry based on old Romanian ballads: "Miorita" (The Lamb)
Slaveykov, Petko	1827-1895	Bulgaria's first outstanding poet
Creangă, Ion	1837-1889	Romanian. Stories: *Amintiri din copilarie* (Childhood Reminiscences)
Drumev, Vasil	1841-1901	Bulgarian. Play: *Ivanko*
Frashëri, Naim	1846-1900	Albanian. Pastoral idyll: *Bagëti e Bujqësi* (Cattle and Land)
Botev, Khristo	1847-1876	Bulgarian. Patriotic poems and ballads
Eminescu, Mihai (Mihai Eminovici)	1850-1889	Romania's greatest poet, who drew on both Eastern and Western sources for inspiration. Lyrical poem: "Evening Star." Also wrote novels and philosophical tales
Vazov, Ivan	1850-1921	Bulgaria's outstanding literary figure. Novel: *Under the Yoke*. Plays: *Vagabonds, Borislav, Ivaylo*. Poetry: *Pod nashete nebe* (Under Our Heaven), *Pesni za Makedoniya* (Songs for Macedonia), *Ne shte zagine* (It Will Not Perish)
Lazarević, Laza	1851-1890	Serbian. Short stories inspired by those of the Russian masters
Caragiale, Ion Luca	1852-1912	Romanian. Plays, especially satires: *De ale carnavalului* (Carnival Adventures), *O scrisoare pierdută* (Lost Letter)
Roman, Ronetti	1853-1908	Roman. Drama: *Manasse (New Lamps for Old)*
Vojnović, Ivo	1857-1929	Croatian. Drama: *A Trilogy of Dubrovnik*
Ilić, Vojislav J.	1860-1894	Serbian. Poetry on classical themes, rich in imagery and musical effects
Nušić, Branislav	1864-1938	Yugoslav. Plays, particularly comedies such as *Gospodja Ministarka* (The Minister's Wife)
Slaveykov, Pencho	1866-1912	Bulgarian. Poetry: *Song of Blood*. Leader of a movement to modernize and "Europeanize" Bulgarian literature
Coşbuc, George	1866-1918	Romanian. Poetry: "The Mother"
Fishta, Gjergj	1871-1940	Albanian. Poetry: *Lahuta e Malcís* (The Lute of the Mountains)
Iorga, Nicolae	1871-1940	Romanian. History
Dučić, Jovan	1871-1943	Yugoslav. Poetry: "Jadranski soneti" (Adriatic Sonnets), "Carski soneti" (Imperial Sonnets). Also travel essays and letters
Cankar, Ivan	1876-1918	Slovenian. Novels, plays, poetry, short stories. He created a new, sonorous language and rhythmic style, besides influencing political attitudes

Nazor, Vladimir	1876-1949	Yugoslav. Poetry, short stories, novels, essays
Elin Pelin (Dimitar Ivanov)	1878-1949	Bulgarian. Short stories of peasant life
Yovkov, Yordan (Yordan Stefanov)	1880-1938	Bulgarian. Short stories and plays about life in his native province of Dobrudja
Liliev, Nikolay	1885-1960	Bulgarian. Poetry and literary criticism
Andrić, Ivo	1892-	Yugoslav. Novels: *The Bridge on the Drina, Bosnian Story*. Also short stories
Krleža, Miroslav	1893-	Yugoslav. Poetry: *The Ballad of Petrica Kerempuh*. Novel: *The Return of Philip Latinovicz*. Plays: trilogy of the Glembay family
Djilas, Milovan	1911-	Yugoslav. Political works: *Conversations with Stalin, The New Class, Land Without Justice*
Ionesco, Eugène	1912-	Romanian. Plays: *Rhinoceros, The Chairs, The Bald Soprano*
Kovačić, Ivan	1913-1943	Yugoslav. Poetry: *Jama* (The Pit)
Dumitriu, Petru	1924-	Romanian. Novels: *Family Jewels, Incognito*
Bulatovic, Miodrag	1930-	Yugoslav. Novel: *The Red Cock Flies to Heaven*
Popescu, Dumitru Radu	1935-	Romanian. Short stories: *The Blue Lion*

MUSIC

Mokranjac, Stevan	1855-1914	Serbian. Choral works: *Rukoveti* (Bouquets). Church music
Golestan, Stan	1875-1956	Romanian. A moving force in the new school of Romanian music. Composed chamber music and orchestral works
Enesco (Enescu), Georges	1881-1955	Romania's master musician. Violin virtuoso, teacher and composer. Opera: *Oedipe*. *Romanian Rhapsodies*, symphonies, orchestral suites, sonatas, songs
Hristić, Stevan	1885-1958	Yugoslav. Conductor and composer. Ballet: *The Ohrid Legend*. Choral works, incidental music for plays and films
Alessandrescu, Alfred	1893-1959	Romanian. Conductor and composer. Symphonic poem: *Acteon*. Orchestral works, chamber music, songs
Gotovac, Jakov	1895-	Yugoslav. Conductor and composer. Opera: *Ero from the Other World*. Choral and chamber music
Vladigerov, Panchu	1899-	Bulgarian. Opera: *Tsar Kaloyan*. *Bulgarian Rhapsody* for orchestra, Piano Concerto, Violin Concerto
Lipatti, Dinu	1917-1950	Romanian. Pianist and composer. Symphonic suite: *Satarii*. Works for piano and orchestra
Kelemen, Milko	1924-	Yugoslav. Contemporary compositions

ART AND ARCHITECTURE

Buvina	13th Century	Croatian. Sculpture: doorway of Split Cathedral
Radovan	fl.1240	Croatian. Sculpture: "Radovan's Portal" of Trogir Cathedral
Fra Vid of Kotor	fl.1327-1335	Croatian. Architecture: Dečani church near Peć, Yugoslavia
Juraj Dalmatinac	15th Century	Croatian. Architecture: Sibenik Cathedral. Other architectural and sculptural works in Dalmatia and the Papal State
Clovio, Giulio (Julije Klović)	1498-1578	Croatian. Miniatures and book illuminations
Zograv, Zakhari	1810-1861	Bulgarian. Icon paintings
Aman, Theodor	1831-1891	Romanian. Line drawings, historical, genre and portrait paintings. He organized periodic exhibitions of living Romanian artists
Grigorescu, Nicolae	1838-1907	Romania's "old master." Romantic paintings of shepherds, gypsies, peasant life and landscapes: *The Jew and the Goose, Old Woman Darning*
Andreescu, Ion	1850-1882	Romanian. Landscapes, portraits and still lifes, similar in style to Grigorescu, but more somber in tone
Luchian, Ştefan	1868-1916	Romanian. Founder of the 20th Century school of Romanian painting. His principal theme was peasant life
Pallady, Theodor	1871-1956	Romanian. Impressionist paintings: self-portrait, landscapes, flowers, with a special feel for color
Petrović, Nadežda	1873-1915	Serbian. Impressionist paintings with torchlike colors and quick, rhythmic brushstrokes
Brancusi, Constantin	1876-1957	Romanian. Pioneer and great master of modern sculpture. Among his works, which he reduced to essential forms, are: *Bird in Space*, in polished bronze; *Mademoiselle Pogany, The Beginning of the World, White Seal*, in marble; *The Kiss*, in limestone
Rosandić, Toma	1878-1958	Yugoslav. Sculpture in wood: *La Pucelle*
Meštrović, Ivan	1883-1962	Yugoslavia's most outstanding artist. He led a national renaissance in sculpture. Among his numerous international works are the Church of the Holy Cross in Split, with 30 wood reliefs and large crucifix; the Racić mausoleum at Cavtat in Yugoslavia; bronze Indian riders in Chicago; and the marble *Pietà* at the University of Notre Dame, South Bend
Pascin, Jules	1885-1930	Bulgarian. Delicate, light-tinted paintings of nudes
Dobrović, Petar	1890-1942	Yugoslav. Brilliantly colored landscapes, influenced by Cézanne
Kršinić, Frano	1897-	Yugoslav. Sculpture: graceful, charming marble figures
Augustinčić, Antun	1900-	Yugoslav. Sculpture: the *Messenger of Peace* in New York
Brauner, Victor	1903-1966	Romanian. Surrealistic paintings
Lubarda, Petar	1907-	Yugoslav. Colorful abstract paintings which retain their link with nature: *Resonance from the Universe, Motifs from Brazil, Fish*
Stupica, Gabrijel	1913-	Yugoslav. Paintings with luminous, doll-like figures: *Child with Toys, The Vender*
Generalić, Ivan	1914-	Yugoslav. Primitive paintings: *Funeral of Stef Halaček, Stag in the Woods*
Stančić, Miljenko	1926-	Yugoslav. Dream-world paintings set in ghostly stillness: *Dead Child, Wedding*

Credits

The sources for the illustrations in this book appear below. Credits for pictures from left to right are separated by commas, from top to bottom by dashes.

Cover—Carl Mydans
8—Paul Schutzer
11—Map by Rafael Palacios
14, 15—Dan Weiner
  except bottom
  right; Paul Schutzer
16—Paul Schutzer
17 through 22—Carl Mydans
27—Map by Rafael Palacios
31 through 38—Carl Mydans
39—Paul Schutzer
40, 41—Carl Mydans
42, 43—Dominique Berretty
45—Historisches Bildarchiv
  Handke-Bad Berneck
50, 51—Dominique Berretty
52, 53—Dominique Berretty except
  bottom left; Goskin Sipahioglo
  from Black Star
54, 55—Paul Schutzer
56, 57—John Phillips
61—Map by Rafael Palacios
66, 67—Rista Marjanovic
  Photoreporter, Bilderdienst

Suddeutscher Verlag,
  Bildarchiv der Osterreichischen
  National Bibliothek—United
  Press Movietone News, Fox
  Movietone News
68—Wide World Photos
69—Alfred Eisenstaedt, Baron for
  TIME—Wide World Photos
70, 71—left; Tom Lambert, center; John Phillips right; Wide
  World Photos
72, 73—David Douglas Duncan,
  Bulgarian Telegraph Agency,
  Eastfoto—Eastfoto
74, 75—James Burke
81—Dan Weiner
82—Carl Mydans
83—Bulgarian Telegraph Agency
84, 85—Dan Weiner except bottom
  right; Paul Schutzer
86 through 90—Carl Mydans
97—Service d'Informations
  Yugoslavic
98 through 102—Carl Mydans

105—From "Albania: The Last
  Marxist Paradise" by James
  Cameron in *The Atlantic,*
  June 1963
110—Dan Weiner
111—Jerry Cooke
112 through 115—Carl Mydans
116 through 119—Paul Schutzer
120, 121—Mladen Todoric
125—Lazar Vujaklija, composition
  in oil 1954
128, 129—Jerry Bauer, Klara S.
  Kyrkogata, Karsh, Ottawa
130—Bernard Moosbrugger—Wide
  World Photos
131—Courtesy Harry N. Abrams,
  Inc.
132, 133—Sonja Bullaty and
  Angelo Lomeo
134—Carl Mydans
140, 141—Dan Weiner
142, 143, 144—Carl Mydans
149—Paul Schutzer
150, 151—Carl Mydans

ACKNOWLEDGMENTS

The editors express their appreciation to Henry L. Roberts, Professor of History and Director of the Program on East Central Europe, Columbia University, who read and commented on the entire text; the Free Europe Committee, Inc., whose editors helped with comments and information; Peter Charanis, Professor of History, Rutgers University; and Ann Perkins, Lecturer in Archeology, Yale University.

156

Index

✕✕✕

Production staff for Time Incorporated

John L. Hallenbeck (Vice President and Director of Production)

Robert E. Foy, Caroline Ferri and Robert E. Fraser

Text photocomposed under the direction of

Albert J. Dunn and Arthur J. Dunn

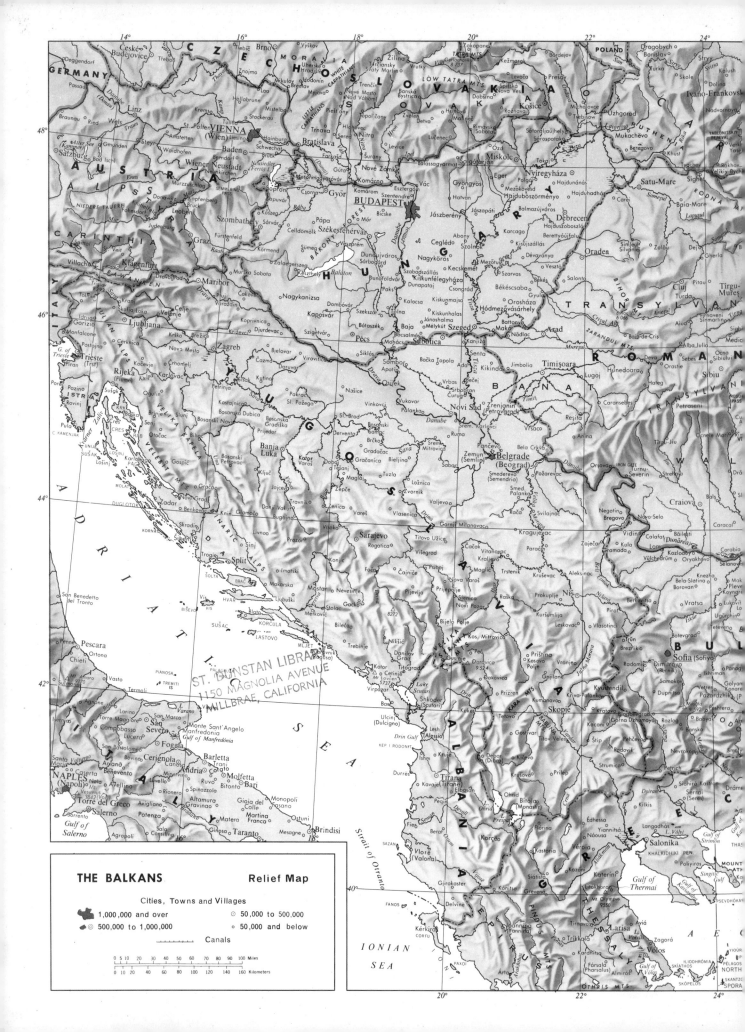

THE BALKANS   Relief Map

Cities, Towns and Villages

1,000,000 and over   ◎ 50,000 to 500,000

◉ 500,000 to 1,000,000   ○ 50,000 and below

Canals

0 5 10 20   30 40 50 60 70 80 90 100 Miles

0 10 20   40   60   80   100   120 140 160 Kilometers